SATCHEL PAIGE

SATCHEL PAIGE

David Shirley

CHELSEA HOUSE PUBLISHERS
New York   Philadelphia

Chelsea House Publishers
Editor-in-Chief Richard S. Papale
Executive Managing Editor Karyn Gullen Browne
Copy Chief Philip Koslow
Picture Editor Adrian G. Allen
Art Director Nora Wertz
Manufacturing Director Gerald Levine
Systems Manager Lindsey Ottman
Production Coordinator Marie Claire Cebrián-Ume

Black Americans of Achievement
Senior Editor Richard Rennert

Staff for SATCHEL PAIGE
Copy Editor Danielle Janusz
Editorial Assistant Nicole Greenblatt
Designer Diana Blume
Picture Researcher Alan Gottlieb
Cover Illustration Daniel O'Leary

3 5 7 9 8 6 4 2

Library of Congress Cataloging-in-Publication Data
Shirley, David, 1955–
    Satchel Paige, baseball great/David Shirley
      p. cm.—(Black Americans of achievement)
    Includes bibliographical references and index.
Describes the life and times of the Hall of Fame pitcher who gained
wide-spread recognition in the Negro American Leagues before
becoming the first black pitcher in the American League.
ISBN   0-7910-1880-6
        0-7910-1983-7 (pbk.)
  1. Paige, Leroy, 1906–1982.—Juvenile literature. 2. Baseball
players—United States—Juvenile Literature. [1. Paige, Leroy,
1906–1982. 2. Baseball players. 3. Afro-Americans—Biography.]
I. Title. II. Series.
GV865.P3S55 1993   92-21058
796.357'092—dc20   CIP
[B]

Frontispiece: *Satchel Paige in the
uniform of the team he played with
most often, the Kansas City
Monarchs.*

CONTENTS

On Achievement   8
Coretta Scott King

1
"If You Were Only White . . ."   11

2
Stuck Inside of Mobile   25

3
"Baseball Had To Be the Way"   35

4
"The Pitcher with the Greatest Stuff"   45

5
A Miraculous Recovery   57

6
"This Was for Keeps"   67

7
"Me and Baseball Is Through"   77

8
The Grand Old Man of Baseball   87

Appendix: Career Statistics   95

Chronology   96

Further Reading   98

Index   99

BLACK AMERICANS OF ACHIEVEMENT

HENRY AARON
baseball great

KAREEM ABDUL-JABBAR
basketball great

RALPH ABERNATHY
civil rights leader

ALVIN AILEY
choreographer

MUHAMMAD ALI
heavyweight champion

RICHARD ALLEN
*religious leader and
social activist*

MAYA ANGELOU
author

LOUIS ARMSTRONG
musician

ARTHUR ASHE
tennis great

JOSEPHINE BAKER
entertainer

JAMES BALDWIN
author

BENJAMIN BANNEKER
scientist and mathematician

AMIRI BARAKA
poet and playwright

COUNT BASIE
bandleader and composer

ROMARE BEARDEN
artist

JAMES BECKWOURTH
frontiersman

MARY MCLEOD BETHUNE
educator

JULIAN BOND
civil rights leader and politician

GWENDOLYN BROOKS
poet

JIM BROWN
football great

BLANCHE BRUCE
politician

RALPH BUNCHE
diplomat

STOKELY CARMICHAEL
civil rights leader

GEORGE WASHINGTON
CARVER
botanist

RAY CHARLES
musician

CHARLES CHESNUTT
author

JOHN COLTRANE
musician

BILL COSBY
entertainer

PAUL CUFFE
merchant and abolitionist

COUNTEE CULLEN
poet

BENJAMIN DAVIS, SR., AND
BENJAMIN DAVIS, JR.
military leaders

SAMMY DAVIS, JR.
entertainer

FATHER DIVINE
religious leader

FREDERICK DOUGLASS
abolitionist editor

CHARLES DREW
physician

W. E. B. DU BOIS
scholar and activist

PAUL LAURENCE DUNBAR
poet

KATHERINE DUNHAM
dancer and choreographer

DUKE ELLINGTON
bandleader and composer

RALPH ELLISON
author

JULIUS ERVING
basketball great

JAMES FARMER
civil rights leader

ELLA FITZGERALD
singer

MARCUS GARVEY
black nationalist leader

JOSH GIBSON
baseball great

DIZZY GILLESPIE
musician

ALEX HAILEY
author

PRINCE HALL
social reformer

WILLIAM HASTIE
educator and politician

MATTHEW HENSON
explorer

CHESTER HIMES
author

BILLIE HOLIDAY
singer

JOHN HOPE
educator

LENA HORNE
entertainer

LANGSTON HUGHES
poet

ZORA NEALE HURSTON
author

JESSE JACKSON
civil rights leader and politician

MICHAEL JACKSON
entertainer

JACK JOHNSON
heavyweight champion

JAMES WELDON JOHNSON
author

MAGIC JOHNSON
basketball great

SCOTT JOPLIN
composer

BARBARA JORDAN
politician

CORETTA SCOTT KING
civil rights leader

MARTIN LUTHER KING, JR.
civil rights leader

LEWIS LATIMER
scientist

SPIKE LEE
filmmaker

REGINALD LEWIS
entrepreneur

ALAIN LOCKE
scholar and educator

JOE LOUIS
heavyweight champion

RONALD MCNAIR
astronaut

MALCOLM X
militant black leader

THURGOOD MARSHALL
Supreme Court justice

TONI MORRISON
author

CONSTANCE BAKER
MOTLEY
*civil rights leader
and judge*

ELIJAH MUHAMMAD
religious leader

EDDIE MURPHY
entertainer

JESSE OWENS
champion athlete

SATCHEL PAIGE
baseball great

CHARLIE PARKER
musician

GORDON PARKS
photographer

ROSA PARKS
civil rights leader

SIDNEY POITIER
actor

ADAM CLAYTON
POWELL, JR.
political leader

COLIN POWELL
military leader

LEONTYNE PRICE
opera singer

A. PHILIP RANDOLPH
labor leader

PAUL ROBESON
singer and actor

JACKIE ROBINSON
baseball great

DIANA ROSS
entertainer

BILL RUSSELL
basketball great

JOHN RUSSWURM
publisher

SOJOURNER TRUTH
antislavery activist

HARRIET TUBMAN
antislavery activist

NAT TURNER
slave revolt leader

DENMARK VESEY
slave revolt leader

ALICE WALKER
author

MADAM C. J. WALKER
entrepreneur

BOOKER T. WASHINGTON
educator and racial spokesman

IDA WELLS-BARNETT
civil rights leader

WALTER WHITE
civil rights leader

OPRAH WINFREY
entertainer

STEVIE WONDER
musician

RICHARD WRIGHT
author

ON ACHIEVEMENT

·◊·

Coretta Scott King

Before you begin this book, I hope you will ask yourself what the word *excellence* means to you. I think that it's a question we should all ask, and keep asking as we grow older and change. Because the truest answer to it should never change. When you think of excellence, perhaps you think of success at work; or of becoming wealthy; or meeting the right person, getting married, and having a good family life.

Those important goals are worth striving for, but there is a better way to look at excellence. As Martin Luther King, Jr., said in one of his last sermons, "I want you to be first in love. I want you to be first in moral excellence. I want you to be first in generosity. If you want to be important, wonderful. If you want to be great, wonderful. But recognize that he who is greatest among you shall be your servant."

My husband, Martin Luther King, Jr., knew that the true meaning of achievement is service. When I met him, in 1952, he was already ordained as a Baptist preacher and was working toward a doctoral degree at Boston University. I was studying at the New England Conservatory and dreamed of accomplishments in music. We married a year later, and after I graduated the following year we moved to Montgomery, Alabama. We didn't know it then, but our notions of achievement were about to undergo a dramatic change.

You may have read or heard about what happened next. What began with the boycott of a local bus line grew into a national movement, and by the time he was assassinated in 1968 my husband had fashioned a black movement powerful enough to shatter forever the practice of racial segregation. What you may not have read about is where he got his method for resisting injustice without compromising his religious beliefs.

He adopted the strategy of nonviolence from a man of a different race, who lived in a different country, and even practiced a different religion. The man was Mahatma Gandhi, the great leader of India, who devoted his life to serving humanity in the spirit of love and nonviolence. It was in these principles that Martin discovered his method for social reform. More than anything else, those two principles were the key to his achievements.

This book is about black Americans who served society through the excellence of their achievements. It forms a part of the rich history of black men and women in America—a history of stunning accomplishments in every field of human endeavor, from literature and art to science, industry, education, diplomacy, athletics, jurisprudence, even polar exploration.

Not all of the people in this history had the same ideals, but I think you will find something that all of them had in common. Like Martin Luther King, Jr., they all decided to become "drum majors" and serve humanity. In that principle—whether it was expressed in books, inventions, or song—they found something outside themselves to use as a goal and a guide. Something that showed them a way to serve others, instead of only living for themselves.

Reading the stories of these courageous men and women not only helps us discover the principles that we will use to guide our own lives but also teaches us about our black heritage and about America itself. It is crucial for us to know the heroes and heroines of our history and to realize that the price we paid in our struggle for equality in America was dear. But we must also understand that we have gotten as far as we have partly because America's democratic system and ideals made it possible.

We are still struggling with racism and prejudice. But the great men and women in this series are a tribute to the spirit of our democratic ideals and the system in which they have flourished. And that makes their stories special and worth knowing. ✥

1

"IF YOU WERE ONLY WHITE . . ."

The oldest rookie in major league history, 42-year-old Satchel Paige warms up before a ballgame at Yankee Stadium in the summer of 1948. Age, the Cleveland Indians pitcher insisted, "is a question of mind over matter. If you don't mind, age don't matter."

FORTY-TWO-YEAR-OLD SATCHEL PAIGE crouched nervously in the corner of the Cleveland Indians dugout on the evening of August 20, 1948. With his sharp, bony knees pressed against his chin, the fading star stared in growing disbelief at the hordes of fans pouring into the ballpark.

"You ready now, Satch?" one of his teammates had teased him a few minutes earlier, as Paige made his way slowly and reluctantly out of the Cleveland locker room.

"Ol' Satch'll be in there," the pitcher barked back at once, trying to hide both the throbbing of his heart and the mounting pain deep in the pit of his stomach. "Them boys are gonna have their troubles. I'm telling you so." But Paige really was not so sure.

The dark, brooding figure huddled in the Cleveland dugout was certainly no stranger to record-setting baseball crowds or pressure-packed situations. Throughout his long career, LeRoy ("Satchel") Paige had thrived on a day-to-day diet of pressure and suspense—and plenty of fans to watch him. During the past two weeks, in fact, clutch appearances by the veteran hurler had drawn record crowds both in Chicago and in Cleveland, where a new major league attendance mark was again about to be set.

Up until this ballgame, Paige had always managed to take both the pressure and the spotlight in stride, fanning batter after batter in tight situations with an outrageous confidence. But tonight things were different. For the first time in his career, Ol' Satch had no idea what was about to happen.

More than 78,000 people had shoved and squeezed their way into Cleveland's Municipal Stadium on this summer evening. For the ballplayers, sportswriters, and fans who crowded the dugouts, press box, and stands, there were plenty of reasons to be excited. Under the leadership of player-manager Lou Boudreau, the hometown Indians had won their last seven games, which made for their longest winning streak of the season. In the process, the club had climbed its way to the top of a tight, four-team race for the American League pennant.

Cleveland pitchers had also fired three shutouts in a row during the current streak, stringing together 30 consecutive scoreless innings. So a victory in this night's game against the Chicago White Sox would keep the hometown team, which had not won a pennant in 28 years, right in the middle of the American League race. And a shutout would tie the league record of four in a row and give the Indians' powerful pitching staff an opportunity to break the major league record of 41 straight innings without allowing a run.

But more than any other reason, the fans had come to the ballpark to see Paige pitch for the Indians. From the youngest, most impressionable baseball rooters in the bleachers to the cagiest, most cynical sportswriters in the press box behind home plate, everyone in the stadium roared with delight at the sight of the lanky, middle-aged man as he shuffled his way toward the mound before the start of the first inning. The crowd was so loud, remembered Paige in his autobiography, *Maybe I'll Pitch Forever*, that "you

The first black ballplayer in the 20th century to pitch in the big leagues, Paige works a pair of scoreless innings in relief against the New York Yankees on July 22, 1948. He made his first three starts for the Cleveland Indians the following month, and each time more than 67,000 fans came to the ballpark to see him perform.

couldn't hear yourself think. It was all noise. For a minute I just listened."

Shifting his size 12 shoes worriedly on the mound, Paige cradled the ball firmly in his broad right hand. Watching the aging star exchange warm-up tosses with Cleveland catcher Jim Hegan, the crowd yelled even louder. On the field before them was one of the strangest and most wonderful spectacles in all of sports: the sight of Satchel Paige throwing a baseball.

The greatest pitcher in the history of the Negro leagues, if not any league, Paige had excelled throughout most of his career with a single pitch, a blistering fastball that he delivered throw after throw with almost flawless control. But what kept his fans delighted—and opposing hitters off balance and con- fused—was his seemingly endless assortment of win- dups and styles of release.

To the poor batter awaiting the next pitch, it must have seemed as though Paige never threw the same way twice. On the first pitch, he might throw straight overhand. On the next, he would whip the ball sidearm. On the third pitch, he would pump quickly toward the plate from a three-quarters position. While on the fourth—if a fourth pitch was needed—the ball would often sail past the hitter from an almost underhand position.

A lean scarecrow of a figure at almost six feet four inches tall and 180 well-concealed pounds, Paige also intimidated opponents with his vast arsenal of wind-ups. The most famous and controversial of these was the Hesitation Pitch. Paige would pause for a split second in mid-delivery—his huge left foot suspended in midair—before releasing the ball. All too frequently, the overanxious batter would swing before the ball had even left the pitcher's right hand. This sight caused the fans to howl with laughter.

Known throughout his career as the Man with a Thousand Windups, Paige also confused batters with quick pitches such as the No Windup Pitch and the Step-and-Pitch-It. And if these were not enough, there were his constant variations of and additions to his Single, Double, and Triple Windup pitches. When Paige really got warmed up, he would often wind his arm in as many as six or seven revolutions before whipping the ball toward the plate. One sportswriter, watching Paige in action during the 1948 season, noted affectionately, "He winds up in the old-fashioned, armcranking style that went out with the electric automobile."

In his later years, Paige expanded his masterfully controlled repertoire to include both an effective change-up, known as his Soft Pitch, and a wicked curve. But it was his unorthodox delivery that continued to baffle batters and delight record numbers of fans, including those who filled Municipal Stadium on August 20.

Watching Paige warm up, the boisterous crowd was thrilled to see the baseball legend live up to his reputation as the game's greatest crowd pleaser. The fans exploded with laughter at the awkward, churning motions of Paige's long, rubbery right arm. They gasped in unison at the high, off-balance kick of his stiffened left leg as he pivoted on the mound. Most of all, they were mesmerized by the drama of watching such a remarkable display of audacity and talent by such an unlikely-looking source.

People never ceased to be amazed to see the slight, stoop-shouldered, brooding figure on the mound suddenly attack the plate with such blistering speed, perfect control, and stubborn intensity. Even at age 42, no one could put on a show like Satchel Paige, and the fans howled and screamed their approval.

But there was another drama taking place on the field that the spectators could not see. As Paige warmed up, his stomach continued to burn, his back stiffened and ached with tension, and his knees trembled slightly as he pressed his toes against the rubber slab at the center of the mound. Even as he was pleasing the crowd with his antics on the field, his head was swimming with thoughts and emotions that slowly blocked out the noise that filled the stadium.

The veteran hurler had something to prove that night—to the fans and to himself—that was more important than the Indians' current winning streak, more important than the pitching staff's string of scoreless innings, even more important than his team's late-season pennant drive. And he would have to pitch one of the strongest games of his life to do it.

Paige had been called up to the major leagues by Cleveland owner Bill Veeck just six weeks earlier. The former Negro leagues star had first arrived at Municipal Stadium on July 7, his 42nd birthday. Not only was he the first black pitcher in the American League, but he was also easily the oldest rookie in baseball history.

During the half-dozen weeks since his arrival, Paige had been used mostly in relief, starting only two previous contests. In his first start, on August 3, he pitched seven strong innings before being lifted for a pinch hitter with Cleveland ahead of the Washington Senators, 4–3; the Indians held on for a victory and a share of the league lead. Ten days later, in his second start, he pitched even better, surviving a ninth-inning scare to blank the White Sox, 5–0. Following this triumph, his record rose to an impressive four wins against only one loss.

But these performances, as fine as they were, fell far short of Paige's remarkable achievements during his 22 years in the Negro leagues. And his list of accomplishments did not end there. In the off-season, he barnstormed against local and all-star squads across the nation and competed in Cuban, Mexican, and Dominican leagues. Although no official records were kept, Paige appears to have won more games, pitched more shutouts and no-hitters, and fanned more batters than anyone who ever played baseball. In one season alone, he is said to have pitched in more than 150 games, gaining victories in more than half of them.

Paige's detractors were always quick to point out that none of his feats had been recorded in the major leagues, where the competition was much tougher than he was used to facing. He may have fared amazingly well in head-to-head contests with white major leaguers, these critics said, winning the majority of his popular off-season showdowns with star pitchers Dizzy Dean and Bob Feller; but these exhibition contests were always held after the season's end, without the pressures of contracts or pennant races. And the teams involved were usually makeshift squads rather than ballclubs with full regular-season rosters. Paige's performance, suspected many observers, would have suffered greatly in the heat of regular-season major league competition.

A couple of major league stars, infielder Cecil Travis (left) and pitcher Dizzy Dean (center), share a relaxed moment with Paige at an interracial barnstorming game several years before baseball's color barrier was broken. "Paige is the best pitcher I ever seen," the Hall of Fame–bound Dean observed, "and I been lookin' in the mirror for a long time."

For those people who were fully confident of Paige's abilities, baseball's color line made it impossible to prove them correct. Like his fellow standouts in the Negro leagues—especially James ("Cool Papa") Bell, Oscar Charleston, Martin Dihigo, Josh Gibson, and Buck Leonard—Paige grew increasingly frustrated that he was not permitted to play in the big leagues. "I always had to listen," he said, "to that same old sentence: 'If you were only white so you could be in the majors.'"

Paige and his black contemporaries faced a no-win situation. Their spectacular achievements were belittled because they were not performed against white big leaguers. Yet the doors of major league baseball remained firmly shut for black ballplayers throughout their finest years.

Finally, on October 23, 1945, Jackie Robinson, one of Paige's Kansas City Monarchs teammates, broke modern baseball's color barrier by signing a contract with the Brooklyn Dodgers. Robinson

Cleveland Indians owner Bill Veeck was one of Paige's biggest boosters, yet he feared that signing the popular pitcher to break the American League's racial barrier would be viewed only as a money-making stunt. So Veeck chose out-fielder Larry Doby (right), who was 17 years younger than Ol' Satch, to serve as the integration pioneer.

joined the organization's Montreal Royals farm team for the 1946 campaign, then made his major league debut the following season. The 28-year-old speedster wound up sparking the Dodgers to the National League pennant and winning the 1947 Rookie of the Year Award.

Paige felt slighted by Dodgers president Branch Rickey, who had decided to make Robinson the integration pioneer. The veteran pitcher believed that he—not the younger athlete, who had spent only one season in the Negro leagues—should have been the first player to cross the color line. "Signing Jackie like they did still hurt me deep down," Paige said openly of his disappointment. "I'd been the guy who'd started all that big talk about letting us in the big time. I'd been the one who'd opened up the major league parks to the colored teams. I'd been the one who the white boys wanted to barnstorm against. I'd been the one who everybody'd said should be in the majors."

As disappointed as Paige was, he realized that Robinson's success had changed things once and for all. By the start of the 1948 season, two former Negro leaguers—catcher Roy Campanella, a team-mate of Robinson's on the Dodgers, and outfielder Larry Doby, Paige's roommate with the Indians—were poised to become big league standouts, and several others were playing in the minors. The black ballplayer's chance to prove himself had arrived at last.

With this new opportunity came a few risks, especially for someone of Paige's stature. If he failed to perform well in the majors, his reputation would suffer, and so would his ability to draw record crowds on his barnstorming tours. These ballgames were not only his greatest source of pride but provided him with a livelihood. He could ill afford to lose both his shot at major league stardom *and* his drawing power on the road.

Paige's greatest obstacle to becoming a big league success was his age. At the time he signed with Cleveland, he claimed to be only 39 years old. His birth certificate stated that he was actually 42. Meanwhile, his mother insisted that the document was wrong, and he was really 44 years old. To complicate matters even further, a private detective, hired by Bill Veeck prior to Paige's signing with the Indians, said he had evidence indicating that Ol' Satch was at least 48.

Paige's exact age was insignificant compared to the toll that the years of nonstop, year-round play had taken on his power and stamina. Earlier in his career, he had proudly referred to his devastating fastball as his Bee Ball. The pitch was reportedly so fast that it made a buzzing sound on its way past the batter. Sometimes he called the fastball his Be Ball because, he said, it "be where it supposed to be."

By 1948, however, Paige's fastball was just an ordinary pitch. "I ain't as fast as I used to be," he admitted to one reporter that July. "I used to overpower 'em; now I outcute 'em."

Whereas Paige's won-lost record continued to shine, his ability to go the distance had not. During the 1946 and 1947 seasons, he rarely attempted to toss a complete game. He was so popular that he took the mound almost every day, which was something unheard-of for even the youngest and strongest major league pitchers, but Paige usually lasted only a few innings per start. As a result, the 42-year-old rookie's lack of stamina became a subject of heated debate, as did his loss of velocity and his still unproven ability to win consistently against top competition.

In spite of these concerns, Paige jumped at the chance to prove himself with Cleveland. "The guy who couldn't get into the major leagues for twenty-two years because of Jim Crow [laws] was in the majors," he remembered proudly. "Now everybody could see how ten years ago I could have won thirty-five or forty games a season in the majors. They could see if I'm kept out of the Hall of Fame it won't be because of lack of ability, but because of organized baseball's color line."

Paige's impressive debut during his first six weeks with the Indians silenced many of his critics. But the night game against the White Sox in late August, with both the pennant race and the scoreless record on the line, gave him his first real chance to demonstrate that he could master major league hitters in pressure situations, just as he had always handcuffed his Negro league opponents. If he could shut out the White Sox, he would prove his ability to everyone, once and for all. He would convince even his harshest critics that he was and had always been the great pitcher that his record indicated.

Paige knew that he might never have the opportunity to face such a challenge again. "This was my real chance to show all those people who said I was too old to be in the majors," he said later of the pressures that gripped him that night, "who said I never really had the ability anyway. If I didn't show them now, they'd never believe I was one of the greatest of all times. But a shutout would set everybody straight."

Paige's nervousness left him as soon as the ballgame began. He quickly retired the Chicago hitters in order on nothing but fastballs in the top of the first inning. The White Sox threatened to score in the top of the third inning, when Chicago first baseman Tony Lupien walked with no outs and tried to speed his way to third on a single to center field by Luke Appling. But Larry Doby speared the ball on one hop and made a perfect throw to third baseman

Having posted a 6–1 record and a sparkling 2.49 earned run average in 72⅔ innings during the regular season, Paige appears intent on taking the mound for the Cleveland Indians as the 1948 World Series begins on October 10. The veteran hurler met with disappointment, however, for he was asked to pitch only two-thirds of an inning in the Fall Classic.

Ken Keltner that easily beat the sliding Lupien. Paige then settled down and retired the next two batters, leaving Appling stranded at first base.

Chicago's only other threat to score came in the seventh inning, when White Sox left fielder Pat Seerey lifted a hard line drive toward the center-field bleachers. Once again it was Doby to the rescue. The Indians center fielder made a perfectly timed leap and caught the ball just as it was about to smash into the seats for a home run.

Cleveland had already scored in the fourth inning, with Doby singling home Lou Boudreau. So when Paige ambled wearily to the mound in the top of the ninth inning with a 1–0 lead, everyone in the stands was on their feet. Even the writers and announcers in the press box stood up to cheer. Realizing the importance of the game, Paige put aside his usual flamboyance and quickly retired the side in order. He had pitched a three-hit shutout, completely overpowering the White Sox.

Paige's masterful performance enabled the Indians to tie the American League record of four shutouts in a row. And by whitewashing Chicago, he also kept the Cleveland pitching staff's scoreless innings streak alive. The next day, future Hall of Famer Bob Lemon outpitched the Chicago hurlers again, blanking the White Sox through the first eight innings. The Indians thereby set a league record of 47 consecutive innings without allowing a run.

As the regular season headed into its final month, Paige's pitching arm began to tire, showing the strain of tossing back-to-back complete games. The free-spirited right-hander also got into a feud with Manager Boudreau, who had little patience for Paige's off-the-field antics when there was a pennant to be won. As a result, Paige saw less and less action in the final weeks of the Indians' drive for the pennant.

The Tribe, as the Indians were often called, ended their schedule in a dead heat with a high-scoring Boston Red Sox team led by Ted Williams. The next day, Cleveland toppled Boston, 8–3, in a one-game playoff to capture the American League championship. The Indians then went on to win the 1948 World Series, beating the Boston Braves, four games to two. Paige made his lone postseason appearance in the seventh inning of Game 5 and retired the only two batters he faced.

When the 1948 season had ended, the 42-year-old rookie had a World Series ring and a share of two American League pitching records. His own mark for the season stood at six wins against just one loss, and his earned run average was only 2.48. Although Paige did not know it at the time, he had shown even the greatest skeptics more than enough to secure his place in the Baseball Hall of Fame.

Now that Paige had finally achieved his lifelong goal of starring in the big leagues, it would have been perfectly reasonable for him to consider hanging up his glove once and for all. But Ol' Satch had other things in mind. "It's taken me twenty-two years to get to the majors," he said later, "but that first season of 1948 was about the mid-point of my career. There was a lot more to go." ✥

2
STUCK INSIDE OF MOBILE

"**H**EY, Y'ALL, LOOK at LeRoy!" yelled one of the older boys from the loading platform down the tracks. "What's that skinny boy up to now?"

It was a hot, balmy afternoon in the autumn of 1913 in Mobile, Alabama, and seven-year-old LeRoy Paige had just finished school for the day and was already hard at work. A few days earlier, LeRoy's mother had decided that his old job, pawning the empty bottles he sorted out of the neighbors' garbage, was not bringing in enough pennies to cover his share of the family expenses. So LeRoy had found an after-school position at the train yard, hauling heavy canvas bags of mail and leather satchels packed full of supplies from the open boxcars to the depot down the tracks.

The wage was a fair one for the day, 10 cents for each bag LeRoy toted. But the train was overflowing with potential dimes, and the pace of the older boys

A view of Mobile, the Alabama city where Paige was born and raised. His hometown has since produced a number of black major league players, including Henry and Tommie Aaron, Tommie Agee, Cleon Jones, Willie McCovey, Amos Otis, and Billy Williams.

was just too slow for the enterprising second grader, who was already taller and stronger than many of his older co-workers. In a moment of inspiration, he took an old broom handle and some ropes found along the tracks and fashioned himself a makeshift sling, stringing together four of the fullest bags he could find.

"I rigged up the ropes around my shoulders and my waist," Paige remembered proudly years later, "and I carried a satchel in each hand and one under each arm. I carried so many satchels that all you could see were satchels. You couldn't see no LeRoy Paige." Then, hoisting the contraption across his bony shoulders, he began to trudge uncertainly across the dusty railroad yard—much to the amusement of the gang of boys who had just caught sight of him.

"Hey, LeRoy," one of them laughed teasingly. "You look like a walking satchel tree." Soon all the kids were screaming it, making jokes and calling him Satchel Tree, then just Satchel, for short.

As usual, LeRoy's mind was on the task at hand and the money he needed to make that afternoon. He ignored the teasing as best he could and continued to haul at least three or four bags at a time. By the end of the day, he had earned a pocketful of dimes and a new name. "That's when LeRoy Paige became no more and Satchel Paige took over," he declared almost 40 years later. "After that, nobody called me LeRoy, nobody except my Mom and the government."

At least, that is the way Satchel Paige told the story most of the time. Throughout his life, he loved telling stories about himself, especially his childhood in Mobile and his early days in the Negro leagues. And, like his friend and barnstorming rival Dizzy Dean, he was not above changing a detail here or there to suit the needs of his audience or his own flair for comedy and drama.

Some people claimed that Satchel borrowed his nickname later in life, from the great trumpet player Louis ("Satchmo") Armstrong, with whom he shared a similar sense of humor and mischief. Others insisted the moniker referred to his size 12 shoes, which looked like leather bags tied to the ends of his long, skinny legs when he took the mound. But the arguments over his nickname were nothing compared to the repeated disagreements over the actual date of his birth.

One cause for the arguments was the absence of a birth certificate, which Satchel claimed was lost when the family Bible in which it had been hidden was eaten by a neighbor's goat. Over the years, he would change his age to fit the occasion, often over

Paige's first brush with whites on a baseball field took place during his teens, when he worked as a groundskeeper for the Mobile Bears of the Southern Association. By that time, blacks had been banned from the major and minor leagues for more than two decades.

and against the evidence of journalists, coaches, and former teammates. Once, he even contradicted his own mother, who had insisted that her son was two years older than he was claiming at the time. "She was in her nineties when she told the reporter that," cautioned Satchel, "and sometimes she tended to forget things."

When Paige made his major league debut with the Cleveland Indians in 1948, most people accepted his claim that he was 42 years old. Six years later, when an aging Paige, who was struggling to keep his place on the roster of the St. Louis Browns, vowed publicly that he was "only 44," many people had grown skeptical—even of his earlier, more modest claims. "Satchel sees nothing chronologically amiss in the fact that he has insisted that he is 44 years old for the past three years," mused a reporter in the *Sporting News*. "Insiders with the Browns claim he is nearer 55."

Though no one will ever know for certain, today most people agree that LeRoy Robert Paige was born on July 7, 1906, in a shotgun house on South Franklin Street on the south side of Mobile. The seventh of 11 children, he was born to poor but hardworking parents. Satchel's mother, a proud washerwoman named Lulu, managed the family budget and pushed her children to succeed. His father, John Paige, was a gentle, soft-spoken man who worked as a gardener but preferred to be called a landscaper. He died when Satchel was only 18.

By then, Satchel had acquired the charm, sly humor, and raw physical talent that allowed him to cope with and move beyond hard times. But while he was still a child, growing up poor and black in Mobile was a nightmare from which he would do almost anything to escape. Both of Satchel's parents shared this longing for a better place in life. They even added the letter *i* to the original family name of

Page, Satchel explained, "to make themselves sound more high-tone."

Along with their ambition, his parents possessed patience and restraint. Once, after being severely punished by his mother for skipping school, Satchel realized for the first time that she, too, "must have been chased away from the white man's swimming places. She must have gotten run off from the white man's stores and stands for just looking hungry at a fish fry. She must have heard those men yelling, 'Get out of here, you no-good nigger.' She must have heard it," he reflected. "I guess she learned to live with it."

Living with poverty and racism was something Satchel could never accept. But for a poor black child on the south side of Mobile, impatience and anger meant only one thing: trouble. And from an early age, he found himself in one sticky situation after another: stealing candy and toys from the general store, skipping school more often than he went, and picking fights with the white boys across the tracks.

It was during this time that young Satchel discovered the talent that would later make him a baseball star. A few months after taking the bag-toting job at the train depot, he found a less strenuous position sweeping up the grounds at Mobile's Eureka Gardens, where the Mobile Tigers, a black semiprofessional baseball team, practiced and played its home games. That spring, he spent a lot more time watching the ballgames than cleaning up the stadium.

Satchel was too poor to afford a baseball of his own and too young to play on any of the local school teams, so he began throwing rocks at everything in sight. One evening after work, his mother sent him to the backyard chicken coop to fetch one of the family's chickens for the evening meal. It was then that the future Hall of Famer discovered the remarkable power and accuracy of his long right arm.

"Three chickens came prancing along the path toward me," he said with a laugh years later while recalling the story. "The one in the middle looked the plumpest. I picked up a rock. The chickens were about thirty feet from me. I took aim and threw. There was a squawking and feathers flew and two chickens went tearing off. The third one, the one in the middle, was knocked dead on the ground."

Satchel soon put his newfound talent to use by fighting in rock-throwing wars with the other children in the neighborhood. His accuracy and speed improved quickly with practice, and he became good enough to get himself and his friends into more than their share of trouble. "Our biggest fights," he recalled, "came on the way home from school and a big gang from [the white neighborhood] was always waiting for us. When we got close, the rocks started flying. I crippled a lot of them, and I mean it. It got so bad they had to put a policeman there."

But the local police were not the only ones to take notice of Satchel's arm. By the time he was 10 years old, both his pitching ability and his insistent bragging had gained the attention of baseball coach Wilbur Hines, who conducted the spring tryouts at the W. H. Council School. Although Satchel was several years younger than most of the other boys, he easily made the team, at first as an outfielder.

Satchel finally got his chance to prove himself as a pitcher in the second half of the season. It was a terrible day for the Council School; both of the team's pitchers had been knocked off the mound in the first inning. From his seat in the dugout, Coach Hines could hear the brash, skinny youngster hollering from center field, "Put me in, Coach! Put me in!" And with little else left to lose and none of the older boys eager to take the mound, Hines decided to give the young upstart a chance.

It was Satchel's first opportunity to throw to a batter from a real pitcher's mound, and his inexperience was obvious. "I was all arms and legs," he admitted. "I must have looked like an ostrich. When I let go of the ball, I almost fell off that mound."

But to everyone's surprise—except his own—Satchel was every bit as good as he claimed he was. "The ball whipped past three straight batters for strikeouts," he recalled. "I kept pumping for eight more innings. When I was done I had struck out sixteen and hadn't given up a hit." The Council School, trailing 6–0 when Satchel took the mound, went on to win the game, 11–6. After that, Satchel was given a new position: starting pitcher.

For the next two years, Satchel got better and better on the field and worse and worse everywhere else. The fights, the skipping school and work, and the petty thefts all increased. He quickly became known as one of the best pitchers—and biggest troublemakers—on the south side of Mobile. And then one day he got caught, and his life was changed forever.

It seemed like such a little thing to Satchel at the time. Coming home from a game one afternoon, he noticed some brightly colored rings and other trinkets sparkling from a display in a store window across the way. Satchel liked what he saw, but he did not have even the few pennies that the items cost. So, without even thinking about it, he ran into the store, scooped a handful of merchandise into his pocket, and turned to leave. Only this time the store owner had noticed Satchel eyeing the rings before he entered and had moved to block the door before Satchel could make his getaway.

Before the youngster knew what was happening, the owner was dragging him by his worn-out collar to the local police station. Satchel realized the matter

A former pitching ace for several independent ballclubs, Andrew ("Rube") Foster put organized black baseball on the map in 1920, when he founded the nation's first all-black league, the Negro National League. Nearly as skilled at self-promotion as Foster was at organizing, Paige promptly turned himself into black baseball's greatest drawing card when he became a professional ballplayer in 1927.

was really serious when his mother arrived at the station. She usually greeted each of his pranks with a series of lectures and a sound thrashing. But this time was different; she did not punish him at all, not even after they got home.

The next morning, Satchel and his mother returned to the police station. Lulu Paige sat quietly, crying softly to herself as she listened to the policemen and the truant officer, who had been called in to handle the case. Finally, Satchel and his mother heard them read the court's decision: "On this day, the twenty-fourth of July, 1918, Leroy Paige is ordered committed to the Industrial School for Negro Children at Mount Meigs, Alabama."

Barely 12 years old, Satchel was terrified at the thought of leaving home for the first time in his life. "A kid," he remembered, "is too scared to think at first when they tear him away from his family and send him to a reformatory. It all seemed like a dream until they closed the door on me. Then I knew it was real." More than five years would pass before he returned home to Mobile.

Nevertheless, being sentenced to Mount Meigs was, in many ways, the best thing that could have happened to Satchel. He thrived there. Not only did he receive the strict discipline, round-the-clock attention, and daily regimen that were missing from his life in Mobile; he also got to sing in the choir, perform in the drum corps, and, of course, play baseball. By the time he turned 15, he had already reached his adult height of six feet three and a half inches; and at a mere 140 pounds, he was certainly an imposing, if somewhat comical, figure on the mound.

"That tall, skinny look helped out," he recalled. "My coach [at Mount Meigs] showed me how to kick up my foot so it looked like I'd blacked out the sky.

And he showed me how to swing my arm around so it looked like I let go of the ball when my hand was right in the batter's face."

By the time Satchel was released from reform school in the winter of 1923, he knew exactly what he wanted to do with his life: play baseball. He might be going home to south Mobile, but he planned to leave there as soon as he could. His stay at Mount Meigs had convinced him that he could get out of town by using his pitching arm as a one-way ticket.

"You might say," Satchel Paige said later, "I traded five years of freedom to learn how to pitch." ✥

3

"BASEBALL HAD TO
BE THE WAY"

SATCHEL PAIGE HAD been back in Mobile for only a few days when his mother began urging him to look for work. Times had gotten even harder for the family while he had been away, and his sisters and brothers, all of whom had grown so much that he barely recognized them, were doing their share to make ends meet. They saved the nickels and dimes they earned from odd jobs around the neighborhood.

Paige did not have an easy time finding a place where he could make a contribution. All the potential employers who knew where he had been for the past five years were reluctant to trust him with a job. And those who were not aware of his tarnished record did not seem to have any work to offer. When spring finally arrived, he was still looking for something to do.

It was little surprise to anyone, then, to see the out-of-work 18-year-old hanging around Eureka Gardens, where his older brother Wilson, also known as Paddlefoot, had recently become a pitcher and catcher for the Mobile Tigers, one of the area's all-black semipro teams. Like most semipro black squads, the Tigers had few fans and very little money. During the good times, players earned up to a dollar a game but often had to settle for a cold pitcher of lemonade as payment instead. With no other opportunities for employment and always eager to take the mound, Satchel took Wilson's advice and decided to try out for the team.

The Tigers' seasoned coach had his doubts about the unproven abilities of this skinny, inexperienced teenager with the loud mouth, even if he was Paddlefoot's younger brother. In what was to become Satchel's trademark for introducing himself to a new and often skeptical coach or group of teammates, he challenged the coach to face him in batting practice. Ten pitches and 10 strikes later, the slack-jawed coach gave the lanky ballplayer a one-dollar bill, a pat on the back, and an invitation to the next day's practice.

"That was the point," Paige recalled, "where I gave up kid's baseball—baseball just for fun—and started baseball as a career, started doing what I'd been thinking about doing off and on since my coach at the Mount'd told me about getting somewhere in the world if I concentrated on baseball. And getting somewhere in the world is what I wanted most. Baseball had to be the way, too. I didn't know anything else."

Paige spent much of the 1924 and 1925 seasons pitching for the Tigers. At a dollar—or less—a game, he made so little money that he soon began pitching for other semipro teams in the area on days when he was not scheduled to start for the Tigers. While this was not an uncommon practice at the time, Paige was so skilled at both pitching and self-promotion that he was rarely ever around for a Tigers practice. "The Tigers didn't like it too much," he acknowledged, "but my pocketbook sure did."

The pocket change that could be made by pitching almost every day still did not amount to much, so Paige soon had to look for "real work." He finally landed a custodial job at the stadium where the Mobile Bears, a white professional team, played its home games. The job marked his first contact with white ballplayers, and he admittedly spent more time watching and sizing up the Bears than he did sweeping the sidewalks or picking up the bottles and papers left by the fans.

One day, after watching the white players practice, Paige decided he had seen enough. He felt that he was at least as good as, if not better than, the more experienced young men on the field. Much to their amusement, he began taunting the players from behind their dugout, daring any of them to try their luck against his blazing fastball.

"We went down on the field," Paige remembered proudly, "and one of them grabbed a bat and another a glove to catch me. I threw four or five real easy like, just to warm up. Then the batter headed for the plate. 'No need for you to tote that wood up there,' I yelled at him. 'It's just weight. You ain't gonna need it 'cause I'm gonna throw you nothin' but my trouble ball.' I threw. Them little muscles all around me tingled. They knew what we were doing. The first guy up there swung and missed three fast ones. Another tried it. He just caused a breeze."

And then, in the midst of his triumph, Paige heard for the first time the words that would so anger and frustrate him for almost 25 years. "We sure could use you," one of the dumbfounded Bears players finally admitted, "if you were only white."

According to all accounts, Paige was an overpowering pitcher from the start. His blistering fastball—or Bee Ball, as he liked to call it—made more than his coach with the Tigers and the white players on the Bears look foolish. Just about everyone he faced left their bats resting uselessly on their shoulders as Paige's pitches crashed past them into the catcher's mitt. Although no official records were kept during this period and Paige pitched against players of varying quality, his record for 1924 was a

"Satchel was faster than all of them," fellow Negro leaguer James ("Cool Papa") Bell said of Paige's ability to throw a baseball. And Bell was certainly an authority on speed: the fleet-footed center fielder "was so fast," Paige claimed, "he'd turn the light out and jump into bed before it got dark."

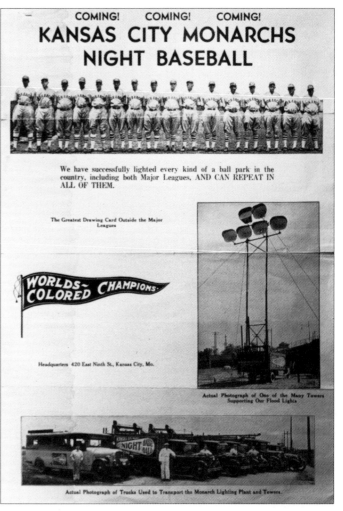

An advertisement for the Kansas City Monarchs, one of the original eight teams in the Negro National League and winners of the first Negro World Series ever held. The Monarchs, for whom Paige played from 1940 to 1947 and again in 1950, went on to become the most successful franchise in Negro league history.

dazzling 30 wins—several of which were no-hitters—against only 1 loss. In 1925, he later claimed with typical bravado, he did even better.

Paige's control was another matter entirely. Years later, he loved to argue that he could throw with pinpoint accuracy even when he was a teenager in reform school, humming strike after strike over a small handkerchief that he would spread across home plate. Many of the players who faced him during his earliest years in professional ball disagreed. "It was worth half your life to hit against him when he came up," remembered Floyd ("Jelly") Gardner, who batted against Paige in 1928. "One time [the ball would come] at you, one more time behind you, the next time at your feet. You had to be an acrobat."

Paige, of course, had an answer for everything. He countered such recollections with the explanation that he had merely pretended to be wild so he could intimidate batters who had never faced him before. In describing one legendary erratic outing during the 1928 season, against Cool Papa Bell and the St. Louis Stars, Paige insisted, "I hit a few batters that day, but I meant to. Why, I haven't hit more than two batters in my entire life except when I wanted to."

Paige spent the first half of the 1926 season with Mobile's Down the Bay Boys, a ballclub that was a small step up from the Tigers. He won just about every game he pitched, and he was soon feeling bold enough for a display of his audacious confidence. With a personal winning streak on the line, he took a 1–0 lead into the ninth inning and quickly retired the first two batters. Then his teammates made three straight errors to load the bases. Paige became furious, feeling his teammates had deliberately let the runners advance because they were jealous of his success. He stormed off the mound as the small crowd began to boo.

After regaining his composure, Paige ambled back to the mound and motioned to his outfielders to leave their positions. The crowd grew silent, uncertain as to what would happen next. "When [the outfielders] got in around me," Paige recalled, "I said, 'Sit down there on the ground right behind me. I'm pitching this last guy without an outfield.'"

Amazingly, the outfielders took their places on the dirt around the mound. The coach of the Down the Bay Boys, sensing the profit-making potential of such a prank—if his pitcher could pull it off—sat nervously in the dugout. As for Paige, he turned to face the bewildered batter and realized for the first time that he had the power to capture a crowd's excitement and approval. It was a lesson the hurler never forgot.

Everyone in the stadium—players and fans alike—was waiting to see what would happen next. "They were watching me and only me," Paige said. "I heard the roar all around. Everybody was yelling. I took my time, then pumped back and forth and threw. It was strike one, but you couldn't hear the umpire for all the yelling. He just waved his arm."

The same thing happened after Paige threw the next pitch for strike two.

"Back I leaned," Paige remembered, "and then I threw. The batter swung but my quickie hopped right over the wood into the catcher's glove. The crowd really went crazy. You wouldn't think a few hundred could make that much noise. But they did."

After Paige had compiled a remarkable streak of 25 straight victories midway through the season, his friend Alex Herman offered him $50 a month to pitch for the Chattanooga Black Lookouts, a professional team in the Negro Southern League. Paige jumped at the invitation.

Herman was impressed by the speed and movement of the 20-year-old sensation's Bee Ball, but he was not so happy with Paige's control. Before Herman would trust the young pitcher against the more experienced professional competition of the Negro Southern League, he made Paige spend hours and hours practicing after the other players had left for the day. Sometimes Herman would line rows of pop bottles across home plate and have his friend throw until he could knock them over, one after the other. On other occasions, Paige was required to fire baseball after baseball through a hole "no bigger than the insides of a man's hat" in a fence across the field. "It

got so I could nip frosting off a cake with my fastball," he claimed.

Pretty soon, Paige had become a standout among the older, more experienced players on the Black Lookouts. He won almost all his starts and doubled his salary to $100 a month. By the season's end, he had established himself as a star, but not before jumping briefly to the New Orleans Black Pelicans.

Paige was lured away, it seems, by the Pelican's offer of $85 a month and what would be his first automobile, a jalopy that he treated as if it were a Rolls-Royce. Because he soon became notorious for hopping from one team to another, depending on which club offered him the biggest paycheck, it appears perfectly reasonable that he decided to switch teams for a car.

Life in the Negro leagues was rough going for the players on even the most successful teams. On road trips, they frequently traveled in old buses, more often than not sleeping either on the hard bus seats or, on the hottest nights, stretched out on the ball field where they were to play the next day, with their bags serving as pillows. The chance, then, for a player to drive around in his own automobile and—on nights

The Cincinnati Tigers were one of the many Negro league teams to share a big league ballpark (Crosley Field) with a major league club (the Cincinnati Reds). Traveling and living conditions for the black players, however, were not quite so grand as they were for the whites. "We used to travel by buses," recalled one Negro leaguer. "Because a lot of times you couldn't get trains to where we were going."

when no other accommodations were available—to sleep in a backseat was just too big a temptation for Paige to resist. Nevertheless, Herman lured Paige back to Chattanooga with what was then a remarkable salary for a rookie hurler, $200 a month.

In 1927, Paige enjoyed another fine year, winning almost every game he started. That season, he also received one of the most outrageous and racially offensive offers of his career. Stan Niglin, owner of the all-white Chattanooga Lookouts, was willing to pay the young star $500 to pitch a single game against the rival Atlanta Crackers. Niglin's one stipulation was that the young black pitching ace would have to let himself be painted white before facing the other team. Apparently, Paige considered the offer, until a furious Herman got wind of it.

Later in 1927, Paige was on the move again. The Black Lookouts experienced financial troubles, and Herman was forced to sell his young star to the Birmingham Black Barons of the Negro American League, one of the most successful black ballclubs in the nation. It was a good deal for Paige. With its huge playing field, the Black Barons' stadium in Birmingham, Alabama, was a young pitcher's dream and a power hitter's nightmare. (Two decades later, the deep center-field fence would prove a constant source of frustration for another young member of the Black Barons, Willie Mays.)

Black Barons owner Bill Gatewood upped Paige's salary to $275 a month. Gatewood further filled both of their wallets by renting his pitcher to other teams in the league who were willing to pay top dollar for Paige's services on his days off from the Black Barons.

By the start of the 1928 season, Paige was rapidly becoming a phenomenon among black and white fans throughout the area. Even though the Black Barons were struggling financially because of poor attendance, there was always a crowd on hand whenever it was announced that the 22-year-old Paige would pitch. "Everybody in the South knew about Satchel Paige, even then," remembered his Birmingham teammate Jimmie Crutchfield. "We'd have 8,000 people out—sometimes more—when he was pitching, which was something in Birmingham."

Admittedly, Paige struggled at times while adjusting to the advanced skills of his new rivals. From 1927 through 1930, he won just over half the games he started for Birmingham. Yet he pitched almost every day of those three seasons, hiring himself out to anyone who would let him take the mound. According to some estimates, he won as many as 60 games annually. His best years, however, still lay ahead of him. ✥

4

"THE PITCHER WITH THE GREATEST STUFF"

F EW AMERICAN CITIES during the 1930s could rival Pittsburgh, Pennsylvania, as a center for black business and culture. The Steel City boasted numerous fashionable shops, restaurants, and nightclubs that were owned and patronized by blacks. The *Pittsburgh Courier* was arguably the finest black newspaper in the country, providing its national readership with a uniquely black perspective on the events of the day. And the city was home to two of the finest teams in the history of the Negro leagues: the Homestead Grays and the Pittsburgh Crawfords.

Gus Greenlee, the Crawfords' owner, was a local entrepreneur who had made his fortune by running an illegal gambling network. The colorful Greenlee fancied himself as a sort of modern-day Robin Hood, using his ill-gotten wealth to enrich the city financially and culturally. Among his proudest achievements were a popular local restaurant, the Crawford

Five of the jewels in Pittsburgh Crawfords owner Gus Greenlee's crown: (from left to right) outfielder Ted Page, outfielder Oscar Charleston, light-heavyweight boxing champion John Henry Lewis, Paige, and catcher Josh Gibson. Boasting a lineup that featured some of the greatest names in black baseball, the Crawfords not only profited Greenlee but brought financial stability to the Negro National League during the 1930s and 1940s.

45

Grille; the successful promotion of a number of world-class boxers, including the light-heavyweight champion John Henry Lewis; and, most significantly, his assembling of the Pittsburgh Crawfords.

Whether or not the Crawfords became the best black ballclub in history after Satchel Paige joined the team in 1931 is a subject of much debate. Many baseball historians maintain that distinction should go to the Crawfords' crosstown rivals, the Homestead Grays, of the late 1930s and early 1940s. The Crawfords of the early 1930s, however, were certainly one of the most star-studded groups of players ever to take the field in any league, either black or white. With such future Hall of Famers as Cool Papa Bell, Oscar Charleston, Josh Gibson, and Judy Johnson on the ballclub's roster, the Crawfords sounded more like a statistician's dream team than an actual group of athletes who played together.

Cool Papa Bell, whom Paige often swore "was so fast he'd turn the light out and jump into bed before it got dark," rivaled Satchel as the most exciting and flamboyant player of his age, once stealing 175 bases in a 200-game season. Oscar Charleston was arguably the greatest defensive center fielder ever to play the game and was finishing up his remarkable career by serving as first baseman–coach of the Crawfords. Third baseman Judy Johnson, frequently labeled "the black Pie Traynor," was a defensive standout whose batting average usually hovered around the .340 mark.

But it was Paige and battery-mate Josh Gibson who became the Crawfords' biggest drawing cards, a fact that sometimes created tension among the other stars on the team. While the two were with the Crawfords, in 1934 and 1936, they formed possibly the greatest pitcher-catcher combination in baseball history. And when Gibson played for the Homestead Grays, from 1930 through 1933 and for most of 1937 through 1946, he was Paige's most feared and respected rival in the Negro leagues.

Observers often disagreed about the quality of Gibson's defensive abilities, with his detractors citing his tendency early in his career to allow passed balls and his slow release when trying to throw out base stealers. But everyone who saw the burly catcher bat admired his gifts as a hitter. According to many of Gibson's contemporaries, he was the most powerful slugger ever to play baseball.

With his squatty, muscular frame and his sweet, fluid, flat-footed swing, Gibson hit tape-measure home runs that even eclipsed those of his white counterpart, Babe Ruth. "He could hit home runs around Babe Ruth's home runs," Paige said of Gibson. In 1930, when he was just 18 years old, Gibson belted the only home run ever to make its way out of Yankee Stadium. It was a massive drive that, according to some estimates, traveled as far as 700 feet—almost 300 feet beyond the left-center-field fence.

Most baseball historians are in agreement that Gibson slugged more than 900 home runs in a career that spanned the Latin and Negro leagues and barnstorming games against white major leaguers. He is said to have clouted 89 homers in a single year and 79 in another. To top off those lofty numbers, he hit an incredible .521 for the Grays in 1943 and posted a lifetime batting average of .362.

Gibson and Paige could not have been more different, either on or off the field. Gibson was intense and soft-spoken, with a slow but powerful temper, in contrast to Paige's nonchalant, light-hearted flamboyance. But the two men shared a deep and abiding respect for each other's abilities, and they became fast friends.

"There's never been power like Josh's," Paige insisted. "He wasn't just a slugger either. He was a high-average man, too. If I had to rate top hitters, I'd

Paige's battery-mate on the Pittsburgh Crawfords in 1934 and 1936, Josh Gibson was as much a legend in the Negro leagues as Babe Ruth was in the majors. "He attacked the ball," Negro leaguer Monte Irvin said of the power-hitting catcher. "He was as strong as two men."

put him ahead of Ted Williams of Boston, Joe DiMaggio of New York, and Stan Musial of St. Louis, and right in that order."

As for his own performance with the Crawfords, Paige learned quickly that his fastball, no matter how outstanding, was simply not enough to stop the more talented and experienced hitters in the Negro National League. He struggled at times, actually compiling a losing, 5–7 record in 1933, while developing the curveball, change-up, and assorted windups that would eventually transform him from a hard thrower into a Hall of Fame–caliber pitcher. Still, he was generally recognized as the finest young hurler in the league, and his won-lost records of 14–8 in 1932, 13–3 in 1934, and 7–2 in 1936 were among the best of his career.

Statistically, 1934 was Paige's best season with the Crawfords. He allowed just 85 hits in 154 innings and permitted only 1.99 runs per game. That year, he was also the winning pitcher in the annual East-West All-Star Game, giving up just two hits and no runs in four innings. And near the end of the season, in a specially scheduled match up of the Negro leagues' two hottest pitchers, he dueled 20-year-old sensation Slim Jones of the St. Louis Stars to a 1–1 tie at Yankee Stadium. A short time after this stellar performance, Paige and Greenlee agreed to a two-year extension of the hurler's contract, guaranteeing him $250 per month.

That October, Paige wedded Janet Howard, a waitress he had met after moving to Pittsburgh. The couple soon discovered that married life was more expensive than they had anticipated, even with Satchel's new contract. As he later put it, "After the honeymoon, I starting noticing a powerful lightness in my hip pocket." The pitcher subsequently demanded a pay raise.

When Greenlee refused to come up with the additional money, the newlyweds packed their bags and moved to Bismarck, North Dakota. There Paige and battery-mate Ted ("Double Duty") Radcliffe joined an otherwise all-white semipro ballclub. Not surprisingly, Paige's deal involved an automobile, a shiny new speedster that he received as a signing bonus.

Paige drew drastically mixed reviews in Bismarck. On the one hand, he enjoyed possibly the finest season of his—or any pitcher's—career. He tossed two no-hitters and more than a dozen shutouts on the way to a 34–4 record; then he won four more games in the league's title series.

Paige, however, also alienated many of his Bismarck teammates. He constantly bragged and complained about their fielding and hitting, which he said did not compare with his cohorts' skills on the Crawfords. On one occasion, his entire outfield walked off the field in a huff, forcing him to strike

In 1935, after playing with the Pittsburgh Crawfords for four seasons, Paige (back row, middle) broke his contract with the team and jumped to the Bismarck (North Dakota) Baseball Club, helping them win the first National Baseball Congress Tournament, a semipro tourney held in Wichita, Kansas. He rejoined the Crawfords the following year but was soon on the move again, playing in the United States and abroad.

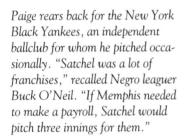

Paige rears back for the New York Black Yankees, an independent ballclub for whom he pitched occasionally. "Satchel was a lot of franchises," recalled Negro leaguer Buck O'Neil. "If Memphis needed to make a payroll, Satchel would pitch three innings for them."

out the side to end the inning. Another time, they let a soft fly ball drop unattended for a game-winning home run.

The 1935 season was neither the first time nor the last that Paige or his Negro league contemporaries abandoned a signed contract for a better offer. Such practices were commonplace, and so were playing winter ball and barnstorming on off days. The reason was simple. With the nation in the middle of a great economic depression, the Negro leagues and the communities that supported them were desperately poor. The owners offered their players contracts that usually promised them little money and almost no protection from being traded or fired at the last minute. Players took what they could, where and when they could. A team's roster often changed from week to week.

With his lifelong hunger for travel and his easy ability to please a crowd, Paige was able to work this freakish economy to perfection. He would pitch year-round, appearing in a ballgame almost every day for at least an inning or two. On a number of occasions, he even led a squad of Negro league all-stars on a barnstorming tour against some of the game's top white players.

Many of these white ballplayers, including Charlie Gehringer and Joe DiMaggio, openly called Paige the greatest pitcher they had ever seen, black or white. Dizzy Dean, who had won 30 games in 1934 while guiding the St. Louis Cardinals to a world title, was particularly emphatic in his praise. "You know," drawled the Cardinals ace, "my fastball looks like a change of pace alongside that little pistol bullet old Satchel shoots up to the plate. . . . That skinny old Satchel Paige with those long arms is my idea of the pitcher with the greatest stuff I ever saw."

Dean faced Paige on several occasions, with one encounter, when they were at the top of their forms in 1934, evolving into an extra-inning classic. Late in this scoreless duel, Dean—a superb all-around athlete who liked to rib Paige about his "weak curveball"—stroked a triple that threatened to end the game.

"I gotcha!" Dean screamed as he dusted himself off at third base.

"No you ain't," Paige growled. "You're not goin' no further."

True to his words, Paige kept Dean from scoring and eventually prevailed, 1–0, in 13 innings.

A curious mixture of competitive drama and slapstick clowning, these highly celebrated showdowns between Paige and Dean and other members of both races drew more fans than a major league contest. More often than not, the black athletes prevailed. Losing performances by the white all-stars proved a source of embarrassment to anyone who insisted that blacks did not possess enough ability to compete at the big league level. Predictably, there were frequent complaints from disgruntled major league owners and numerous attempts by the baseball commissioner's office to discourage integrated barnstorming games or ban them altogether.

Another of Paige's more lucrative enterprises was to bill himself as "Satchel Paige: The World's Greatest Pitcher" and take the mound against the local opposition all by himself, in return for a lion's share of the gate. Teams in other leagues sometimes offered him up to $500—more than many other players earned in an entire season—to pitch a single game. It has been estimated that during the 1930s and early 1940s, Paige made as much as $30,000 to $40,000 a year, ranking him behind only Babe Ruth as the highest-earning player of the era and far ahead of his nearest black competitor, Josh Gibson, who never made more than $5,000 for a year's work.

The most lucrative offers came from the color-blind owners and managers located south of the border. Paige had first played winter ball in the Latin leagues in 1929, when he compiled a mediocre 6–5 record for Cuba. One evening in Birmingham, he explained, a representative from a team in Santa Clara "waved plenty of green in my face and I was packed and down there before he got his hat back on." It would be almost 30 years before Paige would miss a winter in Latin America.

All this bouncing around caused Paige to miss out on the Crawfords' finest season. While he jumped to Bismarck in 1935, the Pittsburgh ballclub won 26 out of 32 games. Then they bested the New York Cubans in a seven-game series for the Negro National League pennant, the only one in the Crawfords' history.

The team's magic season had a calming effect on Greenlee. In his anger over Paige's hasty departure the previous fall, Greenlee had banned the pitcher from Negro league competition. But after the end of

the 1935 season, the Crawfords' owner decided to ignore his own ruling, and he offered Paige a new contract for 1936. Pittsburgh may have been the Negro National League champions, but it never hurt to have a drawing card such as Paige on the roster. He went 7–2 on the season and allowed the opposition a total of 2.70 runs per game.

The following year, Paige left the Crawfords for good. He spent the summer of 1937 playing baseball in the Dominican Republic with a group of Negro league standouts that included Josh Gibson and Cool Papa Bell. Like everyone else in this West Indian nation, President Rafael Trujillo Molina took baseball very seriously, especially when his chief political opponent put together a team of Negro leaguers that embarrassed Trujillo's own team, the Dragones.

Deciding to fight fire with fire, the president decided to assemble the best team money could buy.

Opposed for reelection in 1937 by a candidate who had imported a talent-laden ballclub to their baseball-crazy nation, Dominican Republic president Rafael Trujillo Molina attempted to regain the public's confidence by assembling his own all-star team. Among the players whom Trujillo lured to the Dominican Republic were Paige (middle row, right), Cool Papa Bell (front row, middle), and Josh Gibson (back row, far left).

He sent his agents to New Orleans, Louisiana, where the Crawfords held spring training, and had them follow Paige to his hotel. "Two of them went in to look for him," Bell remembered, "and Satchel slipped out the side door and jumped in his car and tried to get away from them, but they blocked the street and stopped him." Paige was offered the princely sum of $6,000 to join the Trujillo Dragones and was invited to choose eight other blacks to join him. They would be paid $3,000 apiece for the privilege of playing for Trujillo's ballclub.

Baseball in the Dominican Republic proved to be a sobering, if somewhat comical, experience for Paige, Gibson, Bell, and the other black stars. They played their games in stadiums guarded by soldiers armed with rifles and machetes. After dropping a game to the Águilas club, the Dragones were given cause to fear for their lives if they continued to lose and fell short of the championship. Paige and his teammates made sure to gain a berth in the final game.

The night before the championship was to be decided, Trujillo ordered the entire Dragones squad to be locked in jail to make certain that the players got enough rest. The president's game plan, however, seemed to go awry. "By the seventh inning," Paige remembered, "we were a run behind and you could see Trujillo lining up his army. They began to look like a firing squad."

In the bottom of the seventh, Paige singled and Sam Bankhead homered to put the Dragones ahead. "You never saw Ol' Satch throw harder after that," Paige insisted. "I shut them out the last two innings and we'd won. I hustled back to the hotel and the next morning we blowed out of there in a hurry. We never did see Trujillo again."

Paige was ready to return to Pittsburgh for the 1938 season. But when Greenlee offered him $450 a month, the pitcher stormed off in anger. "I wouldn't throw ice cubes for that kind of money," he barked.

Greenlee subsequently sold the rights to Paige to the Newark Eagles. But when the two sides could not come to terms, the 32-year-old hurler signed a deal with Mexico and headed south of the border once more. It was a move that would almost end Satchel Paige's career. •◊•

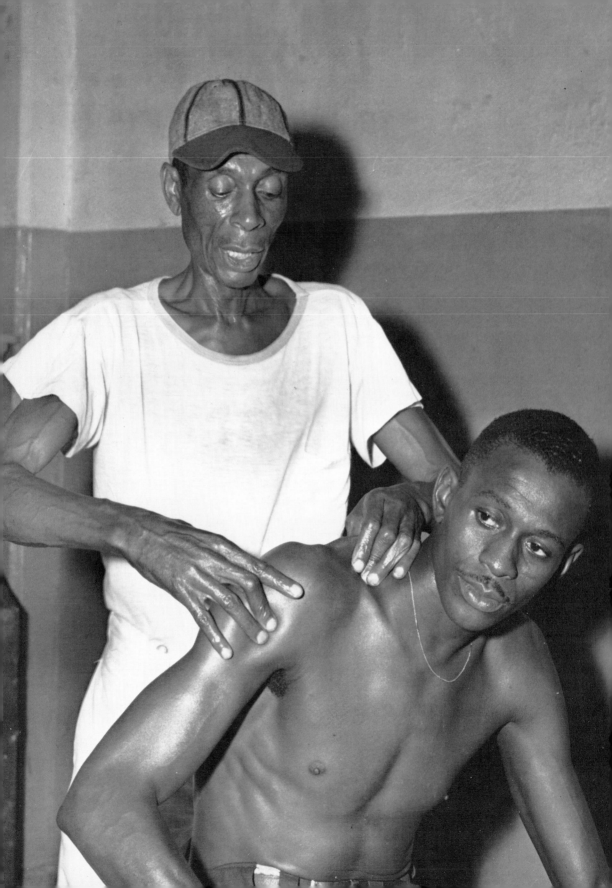

5

A MIRACULOUS RECOVERY

SATCHEL PAIGE HAD been having problems with his right arm for some time when he arrived in Mexico in the spring of 1938. Over the years, he had developed a number of rituals to protect his pitching arm: going through unusually long warm-ups, varying his style of delivery during each game, taking near-boiling baths after every start, and scrupulously applying the snake oil remedy given to him by Dorothy Running Deer, a Native American whom he had met while playing in North Dakota. But the years of pitching straight through the calendar and relying primarily on his fastball had finally begun to take their toll.

Paige was able to make it through his first two starts in the Mexican League, winning one game and losing the other. But the soreness in his arm grew worse with every pitch, until he could only toss the ball from a sidearm position. At the beginning of his third start, he felt something snap. He knew at once that this time he had pushed himself too far.

"I cocked my arm back," he recalled, "but I couldn't even get it up to my shoulder. It was less than sidearm. It hurt like nothing'd ever hurt before, not even my stomach." Then he tried to throw the ball. "All I could see was white. Everything in me hurt. Then I could see clear again. The ball was only a few feet from me."

Kansas City Monarchs trainer Frank Floyd massages Paige's pitching arm prior to a game against the New York Cubans in 1942. Ever since suffering a career-threatening injury in 1938, the hard-throwing right-hander took great pains to keep his arm healthy.

"Base balls are cannon balls when Satchel Paige sizzles 'em over!" proclaims a 1935 Kansas City Call advertisement. All told, he played for the Kansas City Monarchs in three different decades.

Paige thought his career was over at age 32. For weeks, he was completely unable to lift his pitching arm, which had grown totally numb. The Mexican physician whom Paige consulted said that nothing could be done for him—he would probably never pitch again.

Things seemed pretty grim for the right-hander when he returned to the States. His three-year marriage to Janet had begun to fall apart before he had left for Mexico; they would eventually be divorced, in 1943. His habit of breaking contracts and hopping from team to team had not made him too many friends among the owners and managers in the Negro leagues. And despite being one of the highest-paid players in all of baseball, black or white, he had not managed to save any money.

Badly in need of work, Paige sought to become a manager or coach in the Negro leagues, but none of the teams had any openings. He was soon forced to pawn his most prized possessions—including a shotgun, fancy suits, and a car—to help pay his bills. "It'd been a long time since I'd thought about having nothing," Paige said later, "about how it was to grow up in Mobile. Ten years can make for a lot of forgetting. Now I started remembering."

Just when it appeared that Paige's baseball career was over, a pair of very important people entered his life: J. L. Wilkinson and Tom Baird, principal owners of the Kansas City Monarchs of the Negro National League. The two men were convinced that even a crippled Paige could still fill a ballpark. Desperate for work, the pitcher jumped at the Monarchs' offer to join their B team, which was soon renamed Satchel Paige's All-Stars.

Paige's new ballclub spent the spring and summer of 1939 touring the small towns of America's heartland, with the legendary hurler pitching an inning or two at each stop. At first, all Paige could do was lob the ball toward home plate, so he took over at first base. It did not matter much to Wilkinson and Baird what position Paige played. They were right in thinking that his name on a poster was enough to bring in the fans. People swarmed to see Satchel Paige's All-Stars play.

Eventually, Paige tried to pitch again—with unimpressive results. "'How'd he ever get anybody out?' I heard one kid ask his dad after I finished a couple of innings," Paige remembered. "Talk like that hurt you deep inside. Everybody'd heard I was a fastballer and here I was throwing Alley Oops and bloopers and underhand and sidearm and any way I could to get the ball to the plate."

Then, all of a sudden, Wilkinson and Baird's gamble paid off in a big way. As mysteriously as Paige's right arm had failed him, the pain disappeared; he could again throw fastball after fastball.

"That hummer of mine just sang a sweet song going across the plate," he recalled. "It was the finest music I ever heard."

Paige decided to learn a new pitch or two to accompany the music made by his fastball. Cool Papa Bell taught him how to throw a knuckleball, and pretty soon Paige, Bell said, "was throwing it better than I was. That's what I liked about him, he didn't want anybody to beat him doing anything." Paige also added to his arsenal of pitches a wicked slow curve that he loved to throw when the count was full.

Before long, Paige was winning almost every game he started. He was virtually unhittable, completely overpowering the less talented competition he faced. On one particular Sunday, he loved to brag years later, he even won three games: after triumphing in an early-morning start, he won an afternoon game in relief, and then he earned a complete-game victory at night. "I know some ballplayers," he said, "who don't win that many all season." He himself had fallen into that category only a year earlier.

While Paige continued to mow down the opposing batters, the Monarchs' owners decided to let him stay with their B team. After all, the parent club already had a strong pitching staff, and the team was in first place without him. At the same time, Satchel Paige's All-Stars were drawing record crowds everywhere they played. So the traveling All-Stars remained intact throughout the remainder of the 1939 season.

The real test for Paige's right arm came that winter, when he joined a ballclub in Guayama, Puerto Rico. In his first start, the 33-year-old hurler found himself facing his buddy Josh Gibson, who was playing for the Santurce team. At last, Paige would know for certain if he had really regained his old form.

Paige (back row, right) was the main attraction of Satchel Paige's All-Stars, a barnstorming club that first toured the United States in 1939. "I liked playing against Negro league teams, but I loved barnstorming," he said. "It gave us a chance to play everybody and go everywhere and let millions of people see what we could do."

Ol' Satch got his answer when he threw an easy four-hit shutout and held Gibson to a lone single. The catcher had thoroughly dominated the Negro National League in 1939, leading the circuit in home runs and slugging percentage while posting a .333 batting average. But he enjoyed almost no success against his friend in the Puerto Rican League. In four meetings, Paige held Gibson to an embarrassing .188 average.

Paige finished the winter league season with a sparkling 19–3 record, which set a Puerto Rican League mark for victories that still stands. He also posted a 1.93 earned run average and struck out 208 batters in 205 innings. These numbers were more than good enough to lead Guayama to the league championship and earn Paige the Puerto Rican League's Most Valuable Player Award.

White America was finally introduced to Satchel Paige in the middle of 1940, when two of the nation's most popular magazines, *Time* and the *Saturday Evening Post*, ran lengthy profiles on the 34-year-old legend. Both pieces contained not-so-subtle racial

A former teammate who became Paige's greatest rival, Josh Gibson crosses home plate for the Homestead Grays in 1942. Paige and Gibson possessed so much ability that Dizzy Dean once said to the catcher, "Josh, if you and Satch played with me n' Paul [Dean] on the Cardinals, we'd win the pennant by July 4th and go fishin' the rest of the year."

stereotypes (as did *Life* magazine's 1941 pictorial spread, which made him seem more like a clown than a pitcher of big league caliber). The articles were also full of comical inaccuracies: *Time* listed Paige's record for the 1939 season as a superhuman 54–5 and his lifetime batting average as .362; the *Saturday Evening Post* said he was under contract to the Newark Eagles and received a fish fry supper as payment for each victory.

As the first profiles about a black ballplayer to appear in the mainstream, white-controlled media, these articles made a big splash. Coverage of the Negro leagues had always been restricted to the black press and a handful of left-wing publications that petitioned for the integration of the major leagues. Most white daily newspapers did not even carry box scores of local Negro league teams. But after *Time* quoted Heywood Broun and Westbrook Pegler, two of the nation's most respected journalists, advocating the breaking of professional baseball's color line, Paige's reputation—and the public's attitude toward segregated baseball—was never quite the same.

Around the time that the first of these stories appeared in print, Paige moved up from the B team and became a mainstay of the Monarchs pitching staff. His statistical record subsequently suffered because of the way Wilkinson and Baird handled him. To please the crowd, Paige was called in to pitch an inning or two in almost every game. Although he rarely remained in any contest long enough to record a decision, these frequent appearances caused his reputation to grow.

Paige remained with the Monarchs for eight years. Throughout that period, he continued to barnstorm against white major leaguers and to flee to the warmer climates of the Latin leagues each winter. He also alternated between mediocre performances and some of the most brilliant pitching of his career, with the most satisfying and spectacular of his achievements occurring in his ongoing showdowns with Josh Gibson and the Homestead Grays.

The most famous head-to-head competition between Paige and Gibson occurred in 1942, in a midseason game at Pittsburgh's Forbes Field. On July 2, Paige, who wound up pacing the Negro National League in victories and strikeouts that season, was enjoying the upper hand over the Grays. He was nursing a 4–0 lead as he headed into the bottom of the seventh inning.

Paige retired the first two Grays batters before light-hitting Jerry Benjamin cracked a triple. Paige immediately sensed the crowd's growing anticipation. If the next two batters, Howard Easterling and Buck Leonard, reached base, Gibson would come to the plate with a chance to tie the game with a grand slam. The power-hitting catcher was already on his way to leading the league in homers, with 11.

Unable to pass up the opportunity for a classic duel, Paige decided to intentionally walk the next two hitters and load the bases. He walked Easterling on four straight pitches. And as Leonard, a future Hall of Famer, arrived at the plate, Paige turned

Although Paige suited up mostly for the Kansas City Monarchs during the 1940s, he continued to take the mound for other clubs as well. All told, he pitched for roughly 250 semipro and professional teams during his baseball career.

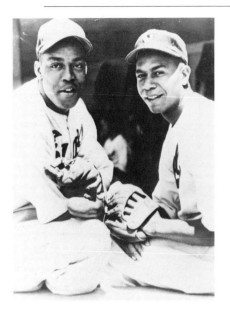

The Newark Eagles' Monte Irvin (left) and Larry Doby (right) were two of the leading candidates to break the major league's racial barrier in the 1940s. But it was Jackie Robinson, one of Paige's teammates with the Kansas City Monarchs, who made baseball history by becoming the first black in half a century to play in the big leagues.

toward Gibson, who had just stepped into the on-deck circle.

"Hey, Josh," Paige barked loud enough for the crowd to hear, "you remember that time when I told you about this?" He stopped briefly to toss the first ball safely out of Leonard's reach. "Now is the time. I'm gonna put Buck on. I'm gonna put him on, and pitch to you. I want this to happen," Paige roared, his voice rising above the cheers of the delighted crowd.

After Leonard had walked, Gibson planted himself firmly at the plate, his cap turned backward on his head.

"I'm gonna throw you a fastball, but I'm not gonna trick you," Paige shouted. "I'll tell you what, I'm gonna give you a good fastball." He fired a fastball at the knees that Gibson took for a strike, with the bat resting on his shoulder.

"Now, I'm gonna throw you another fastball," Paige yelled, "but I'm not gonna try and trick you. Only it's gonna be a little bit faster than the one before." The second pitch to Gibson was also thrown hard, and it was called a strike.

Before winding up for the next pitch, Paige rocked back on his heels and laughed out loud, savoring the full impact of the moment. He had Gibson completely confused.

"Now, Josh, that's two strikes," Paige said. "Now I'm not gonna try and trick you. I'm not gonna throw any smoke around your yoke. I'm gonna throw a pea around your knee, only it's gonna be even faster than the last one." He hurled the ball with all his might toward the catcher's mitt.

As the umpire called strike three, Paige rushed off the field—but not before taking one more poke at the helpless Gibson, who was still standing dumbstruck at the plate. "I told you," Paige said. "I told you I was the greatest in the world."

But as great as Paige was, he would not have the honor of becoming the first black to play in the majors in the 20th century. By 1946, the wheels were already in motion for the breaking of major league baseball's color line. And the 40-year-old Paige was not part of the machinery.

A number of isolated incidents had suggested that it was only a matter of time before a black ballplayer would reach the big leagues. In 1942, minor league executive Bill Veeck had devised an ill-fated scheme to buy the Philadelphia Phillies and stock the franchise with Paige, Gibson, Bell, and other Negro leaguers. (Veeck wound up buying the Cleveland Indians instead and abandoning his plan.) A short time later, Branch Rickey had asked his talent scouts to scour the land for the best black ballplayers. And when Jackie Robinson, one of Paige's young teammates on the Monarchs, signed a contract on October 23, 1945, to play with the Brooklyn Dodgers' top farm team for the 1946 season, the momentous day proved to be very near.

Paige resented not being the first black ballpayer chosen to integrate baseball. But he seemed to take the news in stride; he spoke flatteringly of Robinson and displayed typically good humor while voicing his own undeniable disappointment. To one astonished reporter, the pitcher repeated the same sarcastic phrase he had always used in the face of rejection by the major leagues: "They couldn't pay me enough money to play in the majors."

Paige, however, was probably closer to the truth than he realized. Few major league teams could afford to match the $30,000 to $40,000 he was bringing home each year. Even so, he had waited almost 25 years for his turn to play in the major leagues. And in his heart, he knew his chance would soon come. ✦

6

"THIS WAS FOR KEEPS"

CLEVELAND INDIANS OWNER Bill Veeck first saw Satchel Paige pitch in 1934, in the 13-inning barnstorming classic against Dizzy Dean. Veeck later described that 1–0 ballgame as "the greatest pitching battle I have ever seen." At the time, Veeck had promised himself that he would hire the Negro league star to pitch if the chance ever arose.

Thirteen years later, when Veeck was making plans to hire the American League's first black player, he decided that the 41-year-old Paige was not the ideal person to become an integration pioneer. People would claim that signing the aging star was simply a money-making stunt. Veeck contracted a much younger ballplayer instead: Newark Eagles sensation Larry Doby. The 23-year-old Doby made his big league debut on July 5, 1947—and Paige was denied his place in baseball history once again.

Somewhat hurt and still hopeful, Paige contacted Veeck and asked him, "Is it time for me to come?"

"All things in due time," the Indians owner responded.

The following fall, Paige made a pretty good case that his time had come. In a barnstorming duel against the fireballing right-hander Bob Feller, Paige trounced the Cleveland Indians ace and his all-star squad, 8–0, while striking out 16 batters in nine innings. The performance caught Veeck's attention.

Under the watchful gaze of Cleveland Indians owner Bill Veeck (right), Paige gets himself ready for his big league debut at Cleveland's Municipal Stadium on July 9, 1948. As thrilled as he was to receive the opportunity, the veteran hurler found it difficult to forget all the years he had been barred from pitching in the majors. "Twenty-two years," he observed, "is a long time to be a rookie."

Paige had other things on his mind besides the big leagues. On October 12, 1947, he married Lahoma Brown, a salesclerk whom he had met after moving to Kansas City. Their first child, Pamela Jean, was born in 1948. And in the 12 years that followed, they had five more children: Carolyn Lahoma, Linda Sue, Robert LeRoy, Lula Ouida, and Rita Jean.

Playing in the majors remained his grandest dream, though, and in 1948 he finally got his wish. Midway through the season, Cleveland was locked in a tight, four-way race with the Boston Red Sox, New York Yankees, and Philadelphia Athletics for the American League pennant. The Indians were desperately in need of a pitcher of Paige's caliber and experience, and Veeck's scouts told the owner that Ol' Satch was still the best pitching prospect in the Negro leagues.

Lou Boudreau had his doubts about signing Paige. A strong supporter of integration, the Indians all-star shortstop and manager felt that the veteran pitcher, seemingly near the end of his career and reputed to lack discipline, might prove a liability to the team. Veeck decided to set up an informal tryout for Paige at the ballpark.

First, Boudreau grabbed a catcher's mitt and caught Paige for a long while. Nearly every one of his pitches zipped through the strike zone. Then Boudreau, whose average was near .400 for the season, grabbed a bat and tried to hit Paige's best offerings. Much to the manager's surprise, he failed to make solid contact with any of the 20 pitches Paige threw.

The Indians signed Paige a short time later, on July 7, 1948, the veteran hurler's 42nd birthday. Preoccupied with the pennant race, the normally engaging Veeck was unusually terse in responding to the skepticism expressed by the local press. "Paige was hired," he snapped, "in accordance with our policy of

Paige spends his first night in the Cleveland Indians dugout chatting with the pitcher he called the best ever: Bob Feller. The two ballplayers had befriended one another years earlier, on a barnstorming tour.

getting the best available material, regardless of cost." Veeck reportedly paid the pitcher $25,000—a pretty hefty wage for half a season's work. Also, at Paige's request, the Cleveland owner gave J. L. Wilkinson and Tom Baird of the Kansas City Monarchs $5,000 in compensation for losing the hurler's services.

Paige's first chance to pitch in the big leagues came just two days after he signed the contract. With Cleveland losing 4–1 to the St. Louis Browns, Manager Boudreau called him in from the bullpen at the top of the fifth inning to relieve Bob Lemon. Paige was clearly nervous. "This was for keeps," he told a reporter for the *Cleveland News* after the ballgame. "One mistake, a wrong pitch or two, and my bubble would go pop. My work would be over— just when I wanted to start."

Chuck Stevens, the first batter to face Paige, singled. But after that, the pitcher recalled, "I was just as calm as could be." He retired the next five batters before being lifted for a pinch hitter.

Paige continued to pitch impressively in relief during the next three weeks. He finally got his first starting assignment on August 3, against the lowly Washington Senators. Boudreau, who still needed to be convinced that Paige could do the job, had both

Lemon and Bob Feller ready in relief in case Paige should falter early.

The Cleveland manager need not have bothered. After a shaky first inning, the 42-year-old rookie settled down and gave up only three runs in seven innings. When the ballgame ended, Paige was credited with his first major league win.

On August 13, in his second start for the Indians, Paige was even better, shutting out the Chicago White Sox on five hits. A record crowd of more than 71,000 packed into Comiskey Park to see the legendary hurler. Some of the fans reportedly broke through the turnstiles in fear that they would not be admitted, and 18 people had to be hospitalized.

A week later in Cleveland, Paige received his third starting assignment, also against the White Sox. More than 78,000 fans—another attendance mark—sat mesmerized as he blanked Chicago on three hits, kept the Indians in first place, and extended what would soon become a record-breaking string of scoreless innings by Cleveland's stellar pitching staff. After this performance, Paige's record was five wins against only one loss, with a remarkable earned run average of 1.33. The oldest player in the majors seemed a shoo-in for the American League's Rookie of the Year honors.

As the season headed into its last month, however, things suddenly went sour. For one thing, Paige, who was accustomed to pitching only an inning or two per game for the Monarchs, soon tired under the emotional stress and physical strain of his much longer performances. His fastball seemed to lose velocity with each appearance, and he was knocked out of the game early in consecutive starts against the last-place, weak-hitting Browns.

Paige's erratic behavior also worried Manager Boudreau. Ol' Satch was frequently late for games and appointments, sometimes not bothering to show up at all. On one occasion, after he had arrived noticeably late for what turned out to be a rain-delayed start, Paige explained to Boudreau, "My feet told me it would be a late crowd."

Trying desperately to guide his club to a pennant, Boudreau failed to see either the humor or the logic in Paige's approach to his livelihood. The manager quickly lost confidence in his aging star and rarely used him as the season wore on. Even without Paige's assistance, the Indians captured the American League pennant and the World Series crown, beating the National League champions, the Boston Braves, in six games.

Ever since Paige had signed with Cleveland, the *Sporting News* had been riding both him and Veeck for demeaning baseball with their apparent publicity stunt. Yet at the end of the season, the newspaper gave its American League Rookie of the Year Award to the elder hurler. Upon being told of the honor, Paige joked that he wanted to know "which year those gentlemen had in mind."

Paige and the Indians came back down to earth in 1949. Cleveland fell to third place behind New York and Boston, and Paige's won-lost record dropped from 6–1 to 4–7. He appeared in 31 games but started only five of them. Still, his earned run average was an impressive 3.04, far below the league average.

Even at this stage in his career, Paige could make a good hitter look foolish. In a game against the Red Sox, he went into a double windup and allowed the batter, Ted Williams, who rarely struck out, to see that he was preparing to throw a curveball. "And whoom!" Williams recalled. "Fastball. Strike three."

The next day, just before the ballgame began, Paige went into the Boston dugout and found Williams. "You ought to know better," the pitcher said to him, "than to guess with old Satch."

"Everybody knew what was coming," Paige said of his fastball. "But they didn't know where it was gonna be. If you're looking for it here, and I throw it up there, it's too late."

Banding together with his St. Louis Browns teammates (from left to right) Ed Redys, Johnny Berardino, and Al Widmar, Paige helps entertain the fans between games of a doubleheader in 1951. The drum-playing, 45-year-old Paige joined the Browns' pitching staff that July, two years after being released by the Cleveland Indians.

After the 1949 season, Veeck sold the Indians to Marsh Samuel, and the ballclub promptly released the player who had been its biggest drawing card for the past two seasons. "Paige was just a little hard to handle," Samuel told the press.

Paige rejoined the Kansas City Monarchs for the 1950 season. Like many other Negro league teams, the Monarchs had been thoroughly picked apart by the major league scouts, and they were only a shadow of the powerhouse squad for whom Paige had pitched in the mid-1940s. Fearing that his career was nearing its end, a demoralized Paige struggled with the faltering ballclub. He compiled a 1–2 record and gave up a dreadful 5.88 runs per game.

Veeck came to Paige's rescue. The former Indians owner purchased the struggling St. Louis Browns in July 1951 and immediately thought of Paige as the centerpiece around which to build his new squad. The 45-year-old pitcher liked the idea of being back in the majors.

According to teammate Ned Garver, who won 20 games for the Browns in 1951, Paige "knew more about attacking the hitter from the pitching mound than anyone I ever saw. . . . Paige knew that hitting is timing and pitching is breaking that timing up. He didn't throw two fastballs at the same speed."

Appearing mostly as a reliever, Paige went 3–4 for St. Louis in 1951 and posted a 4.79 earned run average in 62 innings. It was hardly a banner year; 1952 would prove to be much better.

Paige's manager for the first third of the 1952 season was Rogers Hornsby, the leading hitter in National League history. In a head-to-head confrontation almost 20 years earlier, the star pitcher had embarrassed Hornsby; now the game's all-time greatest right-handed hitter used his leftover anger to give Paige a good taste of military discipline. The manager forced him to participate in team practices, arrive on time, and even run laps around the field. "Hornsby and me were from different schools," Paige said, "real different. I guess he wanted to be an army general, but never made it. So he just tried running his ball club like an army."

But the hard work and discipline clearly benefited Paige. In 1952, he was called on to take the mound almost every time a Browns starter faltered—and with the pitching staff giving up the second-most runs in the American League, Paige saw plenty of action. In fact, his second campaign with St. Louis got off to such an impressive beginning that his longtime friend Dizzy Dean, who had become a broadcaster for the New York Yankees, announced on the air that Ol' Satch might be used more effectively as a starter.

"Do you know who I'd pitch if I had one game that I had to win this year?" Dean asked. "If he had proper rest, I'd pitch Paige. He's the best pitcher in the league if he has the rest. And if I was managing his club, I'd have made him a starting pitcher this year. Just think, he'd win fifteen games for you, maybe twenty, just starting once a week. And think of the drawing card you'd have with that guy as a starting pitcher."

Paige became a major league all-star nearly 30 years after he began his ballplaying career, when he was named to the American League squad in 1952. Among his all-star teammates were (from left to right) Mickey Mantle, Allie Reynolds, and Dom DiMaggio.

Hornsby promptly gave Paige a chance, and in his first start he shut out the Detroit Tigers, 1–0, in 12 innings. All told, the 46-year-old hurler pitched 138 innings in 46 games and proved to be one of the most effective relievers in baseball. Playing for a team that went 64–90, he put together a winning record, 12–10, along with a 3.07 earned run average. He was also named to the American League All-Star Team.

Having played in many Negro league all-star competitions, Paige had long hoped to prove himself in a big league all-star game. When he finally got the chance to represent the Browns in 1952, he was un-characteristically open in describing his enthusiasm to reporters. "It's something I've always dreamed about," he said. Accordingly, he was disappointed when he did not get a chance to pitch in the game.

Paige was named to the American League All-Star Team the following year, and this time he finally got an opportunity to take the mound. The ex-perience, however, almost proved to be a disaster. He was called in to face a formidable group of National League sluggers, and it was certainly the toughest lineup he had faced since the Homestead Grays of the early 1940s.

Paige started off by getting the Brooklyn Dodgers first baseman Gil Hodges to line out. But after the Milwaukee Braves third baseman Eddie Mathews popped out following a sharp single up the middle to Brooklyn catcher Roy Campanella, the roof began to fall in. Paige walked another Dodger, outfielder Duke Snider, and then St. Louis Cardinals outfielder Enos Slaughter stroked a single to score Campanella. Next, Pittsburgh Pirates pitcher Murry Dickson blooped a single to score Snider. Paige was spared further embarrassment when Dickson tried to stretch his hit into a double and was thrown out to end the inning.

Paige's fastball was clearly fading by 1953, and so was his effectiveness against major league hitters. Although he could still pitch brilliantly on occasion, his record for the year fell to 3–9, the worst mark of his career. His earned run average, however, was a respectable 3.53.

Paige's overall record in the majors stood at 28–31, with 32 saves and a 3.29 earned run average. He was aware that he had not shown the consistent brilliance of his earlier days in the Negro leagues. Yet he had exhibited enough moments of dominance and flair to convince many fans that the barring of black players had been a huge loss for the big leagues. And it was a good thing that he had achieved this goal, for it looked as though he would not get another chance to pitch in the majors.

Veeck sold the Browns at the end of the 1953 season, and the franchise was shifted to Baltimore and renamed the Orioles. Paige was released from the team a short time later. "Satch, because of his age," read a statement from the Orioles front office, "just wouldn't fit into our plans."

Paige responded to the news by pointing out, "They used to say, 'If you were only white you could be in the major leagues.' Now it was, 'If you weren't so old you could be in the major leagues.'"

7

"ME AND BASEBALL IS THROUGH"

Paige watches a game between the Kansas City Athletics and the Washington Senators on September 21, 1965, from a rocking chair near the A's bullpen. Four days later, at the age of 59, he hurled three scoreless innings against the Boston Red Sox in what proved to be his final major league appearance.

At THE AGE of 47, Satchel Paige realized that his major league career had finally come to an end. No other maverick owners like Bill Veeck were around to take a chance on such a senior ballplayer. Paige was unwilling to hang up his glove for good, however, so he resumed his practice of barnstorming across the nation. For the next couple of seasons, he enjoyed extended stints with the Minot (North Dakota) Mallards, the Harlem Globetrotters, and the Kansas City Monarchs, with his former team now playing all its games on the road because the Kansas City Athletics had moved into what used to be the Monarchs' home park.

Although the 473 innings that Paige had pitched in the big leagues had taken their toll on his fastball, his status as a former major leaguer enhanced his ability to draw a crowd. By the time he approached his 50th birthday, he had become one of the most beloved sports figures in America. Fans filled the stands everywhere he went.

It was only a matter of time before Veeck resurfaced in Paige's life. The promotion-minded baseball man became the principal owner of the Miami Marlins, a new franchise in the International League, and in 1956 he invited Paige to become a minor league pitcher. Tired of his unpredictable schedule on the road, the veteran hurler came running the moment his old boss called.

Paige waits for his turn to pitch for the Miami Marlins, the top-level minor league team he joined in 1956. He remained with the ballclub through the 1958 season and added 31 wins to his lifetime total, which some estimates put at more than 2,000 victories.

Eager to have Paige make a grand entrance into the minor leagues, Veeck arranged for the pitcher to arrive at the Marlins' home opener by helicopter. "They got me out to the airfield where the helicopter was and it looked like nothin' but a big lawnmower," Paige recalled. "The man that ran it showed me how it worked, but it still didn't look safe to Ol' Satch. But they got me in it, and up in the air I was so scared that the pilot and me was like husband and wife until we landed in the ball park. I hopped out of the plane and those Miami fans went crazy."

Don Osborne, the Marlins manager, also did not like the idea of Paige flying into the stadium at first; he insisted it was the type of publicity stunt that would cause resentment among the other players and weaken the team. But Osborne soon learned that Paige was a special case. Shortly before he turned 50 years old, the pitcher tossed a four-hit shutout against the Montreal Royals, the league's defending champions. He continued to stifle the opposing batters for the remainder of 1956, with his best effort being a one-hit, seven-inning stint of shutout ball against the Rochester Red Wings.

Near the season's end, Veeck staged an elaborate spectacle at Miami's Orange Bowl that he billed as "The Baseball Party to End All Baseball Parties." Eight years after he and Paige had helped set the major league record of 78,000, Veeck was eager to break the minor league, single-game attendance mark of 56,000. To bring in a large crowd, the evening's festivities featured lively musical performances by bandleader Cab Calloway and vocalist Margaret Whiting. Best of all, Paige took the mound at the start of the nine-inning contest between Miami and the Columbus Clippers.

The crowd fell about 4,000 people short of the mark. But the evening was not a total disappontment. Paige pitched impressively, blanking Columbus for

Paige is visited by his wife, Lahoma (right), and two of their children at Durango, Mexico, during the making of the 1959 film The Wonderful Country. *Appearing in a movie was no big deal, Satchel said. "I've been in show business all my life."*

six innings before tiring in the seventh, and Miami went on to win the game handily, 6–2.

Most observers of the 1956 Marlins claimed that Paige actually grew stronger as the season progressed. One professional scout, Henry J. Dotterer, gave him a B rating on his fastball and an A on everything else, including his curveball, slider, change-up, control, and poise. "A remarkable fellow," Dotterer noted in a report dated August 6. "Still a pretty fair pitcher."

Paige's numbers at the season's end confirmed the scout's assessment. Working primarily in relief, Ol' Satch posted an 11–4 record with 16 saves and a nifty 1.86 earned run average, the best in the International League.

Always restless, Veeck left the Marlins before the 1957 season began. This time, however, Paige remained with the ballclub. The aging wonder celebrated his 51st birthday by pitching four and two-thirds innings of scoreless relief to help Miami squeeze by Columbus, 4–3. Two months later, on September 11, he made a bid for his first no-hitter in years; it was ruined by an eighth-inning single, and he had to settle for a complete-game, three-hit shutout.

Paige confers with former Baltimore Elite Giants and Brooklyn Dodgers star Roy Campanella on August 20, 1961, prior to the start of the Negro American League's 29th all-star game at Yankee Stadium. By the 1960s, very few Negro league teams were still in existence.

Away from the ballpark, Paige enjoyed a humorous, well-publicized run-in with the law. He loved to drive fast cars and had received dozens of speeding tickets over the years. In late April 1958, Judge Charles H. Snowden ordered him to spend 20 days in jail for two outstanding traffic violations. The Miami-based judge suspended the pitcher's sentence until after the 1958 season, however, and said that he would reduce the jail term by one day for every game Paige won, every run he scored, and "every time he strikes out Luke Easter of the Buffalo Bisons. . . . If he works real hard, he'll come out all right." Paige did, finishing the season with 10 victories for the second year in a row.

In addition to this legal squabble, Paige got into a feud with the Marlins front office, which was trying to find ways to improve the franchise's finances. In August, the ballclub placed him on the inactive list at the start of a 10-game road trip. "It's not for disciplinary purposes," Paige was told. "You just don't figure to pitch much when we're up in the cold climate around Rochester and Montreal." The pitcher became furious when he learned that he would not be paid for this period of forced inactivity. He was convinced that he could still draw top dollar on the road, and he sought his unconditional release from the team. Miami let him go the following winter.

Paige's overall experience with the Marlins had been positive in spite of the recent bad blood. His three-year record with the team stood at 31–21, and he averaged giving up less than three earned runs per game in more than 100 appearances.

Following the 1958 season, Paige headed to Durango, Mexico, where he played a small role as a cavalry sergeant in *The Wonderful Country*, a western starring Robert Mitchum and Julie London. "If I can make the grade," he told his wife, Lahoma, "me and baseball is through." Unfortunately, his great hopes as an actor were never realized. *The Wonderful Country* turned out to be his first *and* last picture.

For the next six years, Paige was back on the road, playing ball. He toured part of the time with the Indianapolis Clowns, one of the few Negro league teams that had not folded after professional baseball became integrated. The Clowns were mainly a sideshow of comics and curiosities, however, as were the Harlem Globetrotters, for whom Paige also performed. His lone foray into organized baseball during this period occurred in the summer of 1961, when he made a few brief appearances for the Portland Beavers of the Pacific Coast League. He did not collect any decisions in his five outings, but he boasted an outstanding 2.88 earned run average in 25 innings pitched.

In the late summer of 1965, Paige's baseball career became intertwined with an American League ballclub owner who was every bit as controversial as Bill Veeck. Seeking novel ways to lure fans to watch his faltering Kansas City Athletics, Charles O. Finley decided to stage a series of "Novelty Nights." The

Paige explains his pitching technique to a quartet of Kansas City Athletics hurlers—(from left to right) John ("Blue Moon") Odom, Jim ("Catfish") Hunter, Dick Joyce, and Ron Tompkins—on September 24, 1965. The next day, in an appearance that marked his 40th year as a ballplayer, the 59-year-old pitcher concluded his big league career.

first of these evenings featured Bert ("Campy") Campaneris, who was normally a shortstop, playing all nine positions in a single game.

To everyone's amazement, Finley's next scheme involved reactivating the 59-year-old Paige and letting him pitch again in the big leagues. The idea intrigued many fans; others were not amused, insisting that such a stunt would demean the game. Paige, they argued, was too old to compete effectively against major leaguers, even in a brief appearance.

Paige had never backed off from a challenge in the past. But this time the aging hurler was inclined to agree with the critics. He said he was confident that he could get the ball to the plate but was "a little concerned about what the hitters might do with it after it got there." Still, he decided to go ahead with Finley's plan.

On the night of September 25, with Cool Papa Bell and several other of Paige's fellow Negro leaguers in attendance, all the electric lights were dimmed before the start of the game between the Boston Red

Sox and the hometown Athletics. The fans held up lit matches and sang a bunch of old favorites: "Darling, I Am Growing Old," "Old Rocking Chair," and "The Old Gray Mare." Then Paige took the mound and put on one of the most extraordinary performances in baseball history.

Facing a hard-hitting lineup of batters who were nearly 40 years younger than he was, Ol' Satch kept the Red Sox off balance with his arsenal of wind-ups, variable-speed pitches, and still-amazing control. In the three innings Paige worked, he allowed only one hit: a double to the third batter he faced, future Hall of Famer Carl Yastrzemski, after falling behind, 3–0, in the count. Paige then bore down and retired the next seven batters. He left the game with a 1–0 lead, although Kansas City eventually lost the contest, 5–2.

Paige was especially pleased with his performance, for which Finley reportedly paid him $5,000. "Everybody doubted me on the ball club," the pitcher said. "They'll have more confidence in me now." But in spite of this wonderful outing, he never pitched in the big leagues again.

Paige made his way back into baseball's limelight in the spring of 1968. Like most of his fellow Negro leaguers, he did not qualify for a major league pension because he had not completed five full years of service in the big leagues. He had missed being eligible for retirement benefits by just 90 days—and that was only because he had not been permitted to play in the majors until he was 42 years old.

Veeck was among a growing group of baseball people who wanted to correct this injustice. "They kept this guy out when he would've been the greatest who ever lived, record-wise," he told columnist Jimmy Breslin. "So now when they have a chance to make a gesture which would say they're sorry, they won't even think about it."

Back in uniform in 1968 as a player-coach, Paige warms up on the sidelines for the At-lanta Braves. Although he never pitched in a game for the Braves, the few months that he spent with the ballclub enabled him to qualify for the major leagues' retirement benefits.

In August 1968, the Atlanta Braves stepped forward and hired Paige as a player-coach for the remainder of the season so he could qualify for a pension. "We expect Paige to get into shape and to be ready to pitch when called upon," stated Bill Bartholomay, the team's owner. Manager Luman Harris added, "I'm going to accept him as a player and treat him as I do the other fellows on the club."

Paige, however, never played an inning for Atlanta. According to Henry Aaron, the ballclub's reigning superstar, "The Braves were afraid he might get hurt, but personally I don't think they had anything to worry about. That old man knew more about taking care of himself than anyone I ever met, and on top of that, he could still throw. He threw on the sidelines, and although this might seem hard to believe, I'm certain that Satch threw harder than some of the guys on our staff."

Aaron, who also hailed from Mobile, was given the honor of serving as Paige's chaperone. "After spending time with Satchel," said baseball's future home run king, "I firmly believe that he may have been the greatest pitcher of all time."

Two months after Paige satisfied the pension requirement, he announced his retirement from professional baseball. Approaching his 63rd birthday, he joked with reporters about the reason behind his decision. "I can still throw harder than most of 'em," he said of the younger players. "But I don't want to embarrass them. It might have a bad effect on 'em."

8

THE GRAND OLD MAN
OF BASEBALL

Paige is all smiles as he is inducted into the Baseball Hall of Fame in Cooperstown, New York, in 1971. He became the first Negro league star to attain the sport's highest honor.

AFTER SATCHEL PAIGE retired from professional baseball in 1968, one question remained to be answered: Would the legendary hurler be inducted into the Baseball Hall of Fame in Cooperstown, New York? Normally, a ballplayer had to spend 10 years in the majors to be eligible for enshrinement. Such a requirement seemed unfair not only to Paige but to the many Negro league standouts who were never given the opportunity to set foot in the big leagues.

Bill Veeck, Dizzy Dean, and a number of other prominent baseball people came forward and said that the 10-year eligibility requirement should be waived so Paige could become a member of the Hall of Fame. Bob Feller stated on a number of occasions that Paige was the greatest pitcher he ever saw. And Ted Williams said at his own induction into the Hall of Fame, "Baseball gives every American boy a chance to excel. Not just to be as good as someone else, but to be better. This is the nature of man and the name of the game. I hope that someday Satchel Paige and Josh Gibson will be voted into the Hall of Fame as symbols of the great Negro players who are not here only because they weren't given a chance."

In 1971, the Baseball Hall of Fame decided to induct Negro leaguers, and a special selection committee that included Roy Campanella, Monte Irvin, and Judy Johnson chose Paige as the first player to represent the Negro leagues. There was a catch, however. The Baseball Hall of Fame wanted to place Paige's commemorative plaque—and those honoring future Negro league inductees—in a special section of its museum rather than in its main hall, where the rest of the members' plaques had been placed.

A protest arose immediately that separating the Negro leaguers from the major league inductees reeked of the same prejudice that had kept blacks out of the big leagues for nearly half a century. "I don't feel segregated," Paige insisted. "I'm proud to be wherever they put me in the Hall of Fame." He had waited all his life for official recognition of his achievement, and he was genuinely touched by the honor, no matter how qualified it was.

Even so, Baseball Hall of Fame officials realized that segregated shrines would only call further attention to the sport's tarnished past, and they abandoned the idea of a separate section for the Negro league stars. Paige was allowed to take his place alongside baseball's other immortals. Josh Gibson and Buck Leonard joined him in Cooperstown a year later. And in the years that have followed, numerous other Negro leaguers have been inducted into the Hall of Fame, including Cool Papa Bell, Ray Dandridge, Martin Dihigo, Monte Irvin, Judy Johnson, and Rube Foster, who founded the Negro leagues in 1920.

As pleased as Paige was to be a Hall of Famer, he did not remain silent for very long on the subject of racial discrimination at the major league level. During the winter of 1972, he spoke at a special meeting of the Old Timers' Club at Cooperstown following the induction of Gibson, Leonard, Yogi Berra, Sandy Koufax, and Early Wynn into the

Actor Louis Gossett, Jr., receives a word of advice from Paige during the filming of the television movie Don't Look Back: The Satchel Paige Story. *Paige himself made a brief appearance at the end of the film.*

Baseball Hall of Fame. Paige dispensed with his usual, good-natured musings and addressed the group in a much more serious tone than anyone expected. "I started telling them," he recalled, "that I thought too many good young black players were being kept down in the minor leagues instead of being brought up to the majors."

White dignitaries made up most of the crowd, and they began to shift nervously in their seats. The assistant commissioner of baseball, who was presiding over the meeting, rose to his feet and ordered Paige to sit down. "This is no place for that kind of talk," the assistant commissioner was heard to say. Paige abruptly ended his comments and took his seat. But he would never again return to Cooperstown, and he would continue to speak out on behalf of black athletes for the remainder of his life.

Some observers suggested that Paige had grown bitter with age. Yet his statements to the Old Timers' Club were consistent with the attitudes he had always held. Although he had rarely complained publicly about how he had been treated as a black athlete, he had never ceased to be angry about all the obstacles he had had to overcome. That much was clear from his 1962 autobiography, *Maybe I'll Pitch Forever*, in which he spoke candidly about the racial prejudice he had encountered during his childhood in Mobile, through his years on the road in the Negro leagues, and in his early days in the major leagues.

As the 1970s wore on, Paige went through brief stints as a pitching coach with the New Orleans Pelicans and the Tulsa Oilers, a pair of minor league teams in the American Association. He also served for a while as a deputy sheriff in Kansas City. He was often asked if he ever planned to return to pitching. To this question, he replied: "I can still get the ball over with something on it—and keep it low. But my legs are gone. They'd bunt me to death."

As Paige neared his 70th birthday, he became the subject of a television movie, *Don't Look Back: The Satchel Paige Story*, which was shown on the CBS network the week before the 1975 World Series began. For millions of Americans, it was their introduction to the ragged glory of the Negro leagues. The actor Louis Gossett, Jr., played the role of Paige. And at the end of the film, Ol' Satch himself was shown suited up in his Kansas City Monarchs uniform, firing strikes toward the plate. His throwing motion still looked strangely similar to the way it had appeared 30 years earlier.

The film drew its title from perhaps the most famous of Paige's many wonderful and witty sayings:

"Don't look back. Something might be gaining on you." This piece of advice was the last part of his recipe for staying young, which he loved to offer to anyone who would listen:

Avoid fried meats, which angry up the blood.

If your stomach disputes you, lie down and pacify it with cool thoughts.

Keep the juices flowing by jangling around gently as you move.

Go very light on the vices—the society ramble ain't restful.

Avoid running at all times.

Although Paige heeded this advice, his own health began to fail in the late 1970s. He suffered from a heart condition and emphysema. Much of the time, he was confined to a wheelchair and had to rely on a portable respirator to help with his breathing.

Relying on a portable respirator to help with his breathing, Paige clutches a baseball during his last public appearance, in which a Kansas City stadium was named after him. "I loved baseball," he was quick to point out. "I ate and slept it."

On June 4, 1982, Paige made his last public appearance, at the dedication of a Kansas City stadium that was being named in his honor. Sitting in a wheelchair, he threw out the first ball before the start of a Little League game. "Nobody on earth could feel as good as I do now," he said to the crowd. "I thought that there was nothing left for me to do. I appreciate this from the bottom of my heart."

Four days later, a flurry of electrical storms pounded the Midwest. The lightning knocked out power lines in Kansas City, leaving entire parts of the region without electricity. Paige was at home that day, and he complained to Lahoma that he had a chill. His wife put a jacket around him and sat next to him. Later that day, June 8, Satchel Paige died. He was just one month shy of his 76th birthday.

As Paige's funeral procession made its way along the roadway to Kansas City's Forest Hills Memorial Park, the mourners passed a group of black and white youngsters standing silently, with their hats off and their baseball gloves pressed firmly to their chests. Many of the star pitcher's Negro league cohorts were unable to attend his funeral because of poor health. But Buck Leonard was there, and so was Monte Irvin, representing the baseball commissioner's office.

Buck O'Neil, one of Paige's rivals from the Homestead Grays, delivered the eulogy. "Everyone was saying," O'Neil told the group of mourners, "'Isn't it a shame Satchel didn't play with all the great athletes of the major leagues?' But who's to say that he wasn't, playing with us? We played the white teams, and we won most of the time. I don't know that we were that much better, but we had something to prove."

Paige, who had struggled long and hard to gain the opportunity to compete against the best, understood that there was much more than the spectacle of interracial competition at stake in the barnstorming games against whites. Back in 1934, both he and Dizzy Dean had enjoyed spectacular campaigns—the best of their respective careers. Yet each man felt dissatisfied when his season was over. They believed that their magnificent performances were somehow tainted because they had not faced one another. And so they sought each other out.

"Diz was one boy I wanted to run up against," Paige remembered. "They were saying Diz and me were about as alike as two tadpoles. We were both fast and slick. But Diz was in the majors and I was bouncing around the peanut circuit. If I was going to get the edge over him, I had to set him down in a little head-to-head baseball."

Paige did, on one memorable occasion toiling for 13 innings before getting the win. At the end of the ballgame, Dean rushed across the field to congratulate his opponent. "You're a better pitcher'n I ever hope to be, Satch," he said.

But they were both better pitchers—and better people—for having played together. And baseball is a better game for having followed their example. ✥

APPENDIX:
CAREER STATISTICS

NEGRO LEAGUES

YEAR	TEAM	W	L	PCT	G	GS	CG	IP	H	BB	SO	SHO	SV
1927	BIR Black Barons	8	3	.727	20	9	6	93	63	19	80	3	1
1928		12	4	.750	26	16	10	120	107	19	112	3	0
1929		11	11	.500	31	20	15	196	191	39	184	0	3
1930	BIR Black Barons												
	BAL Elite Giants	11	4	.733	18	13	12	120	92	15	86	3	1
1931	CLE Cubs												
	PIT Crawfords	5	5	.500	12	6	5	60	36	4	23	1	0
1932	PIT Crawfords	14	8	.636	29	23	19	181	92	13	109	3	2
1933		5	7	.417	13	12	10	95	39	10	57	0	0
1934		13	3	.813	20	17	15	154	85	21	97	6	0
1935	KC Monarchs	0	0	.000	2	2	0	7	0	0	10	0	0
1936	PIT Crawfords	7	2	.778	9	9	9	70	54	11	59	3	0
1937	STL Stars	1	2	.333	3	3	2	26	22	6	11	0	0
1938	Mexico												
1939	Monarchs' B team												
1940	KC Monarchs	1	1	.500	2	2	2	12	10	0	15	1	0
1941		7	1	.875	13	11	3	67	38	6	61	0	0
1942		8	5	.615	20	18	6	100	68	12	78	1	0
1943		5	9	.357	24	20	4	88	80	16	54	0	1
1944		5	5	.500	13	—	—	78	47	8	70	2	0
1945		3	5	.375	13	7	1	68	65	12	48	0	0
1946		5	1	.833	9	9	1	38	22	2	23	0	0
1947		1	1	.500	2	2	2	11	5	—	—	0	0
1950	KC Monarchs												
	PHI Stars	1	2	.333	—	8	—	—	26	28	—	—	0
20 Years		123	79	.609	279	(207)	(122)	1584	1142	(241)	(1177)	26	(8)

MAJOR LEAGUES

YEAR	TEAM	W	L	PCT	ERA	G	GS	CG	IP	H	BB	SO	SHO	SV
1948	CLE Indians	6	1	.857	2.48	21	7	3	72.2	61	25	45	2	1
1949		4	7	.364	3.04	31	5	1	83	70	33	54	0	5
1951	STL Browns	3	4	.429	4.79	23	3	0	62	67	29	48	0	5
1952		12	10	.545	3.07	46	6	3	138	116	57	91	2	10
1953		3	9	.250	3.53	57	4	0	117.1	114	39	51	0	11
1965	KC Athletics	0	0	.000	0.00	1	1	0	3	1	0	1	0	0
6 Years		28	31	.475	3.29	179	26	7	476	429	183	290	4	32

CHRONOLOGY

————— ❧ —————

1906   Born LeRoy Robert Paige on July 6 in Mobile, Alabama

1913   Acquires the nickname Satchel

1916   Becomes a member of the W. H. Council School baseball team

1918   Caught stealing from a local store; sentenced to five and a half years at the Industrial School for Negro Children at Mount Meigs, Alabama

1923   Released from the Industrial School in December

1924   Pitches in first semiprofessional game, for the Mobile Tigers

1926   Pitches for Mobile's Down the Bay Boys; makes professional debut with the Chattanooga Black Lookouts; joins the New Orleans Pelicans

1927   Joins the Birmingham Black Barons

1929   Makes first trip to the Latin winter leagues

1931   Joins the Pittsburgh Crawfords

1934   Enjoys his finest season in the Negro leagues; beats Dizzy Dean, six games to four, in a postseason barnstorming competition; marries Janet Howard

1935   Joins the Bismarck (North Dakota) Baseball Club

1936   Rejoins the Crawfords

1937   Joins the Trujillo Dragones in the Dominican Republic

1938   Pitches in the Mexican League; injures his right arm

1939   Joins the Kansas City Monarchs B team

1940   Becomes a nationally known figure after being profiled in *Time* and the *Saturday Evening Post*

1941   Becomes a mainstay of the Monarchs pitching staff

1943   Divorces Janet Howard

1947   Marries Lahoma Brown

1948   Joins the Cleveland Indians; makes major league debut on July 9; becomes the first black to pitch in the World Series

1949   Daughter Carolyn Lahoma is born

1950   Paige rejoins the Monarchs

1951   Joins the St. Louis Browns; daughter Linda Sue is born

1952   Paige makes the American League All-star team; son, Robert LeRoy, is born

1956   Paige joins the Miami Marlins

1958   Daughter Lula Ouida is born

1960   Daughter Rita Jean is born

1962   Paige's autobiography, *Maybe I'll Pitch Forever*, is published

1965   Paige joins the Kansas City Athletics; makes final major league appearance on September 25

1968   Hired by the Atlanta Braves as a player-coach

1969   Officially retires from professional baseball

1971   Inducted into the Baseball Hall of Fame

1975   Becomes the subject of a television movie, *Don't Look Back: The Satchel Paige Story*

1982   Dies of a heart attack on June 8 in Kansas City, Missouri

FURTHER READING

Brashler, William. *Josh Gibson: A Life in the Negro Leagues*. New York: Harper & Row, 1978.

Bruce, Janet. *The Kansas City Monarchs: Champions of Black Baseball*. Lawrence: University of Kansas Press, 1985.

Chadwick, Bruce. *When the Game Was Black and White: The Illustrated History of Baseball's Negro Leagues*. New York: Abbeville, 1993.

Holway, John B. *Josh and Satch*. New York: Carroll & Graf, 1992.

———. *Blackball Stars: Negro League Pioneers*. New York: Carroll & Graf, 1992.

Paige, Leroy, and David Lipman. *Maybe I'll Pitch Forever*. New York: Doubleday, 1962.

Peterson, Robert. *Only the Ball Was White: A History of Legendary Black Players and All-Black Professional Teams*. New York: Oxford University Press, 1970.

Rogosin, Donn. *Invisible Men: Life in Baseball's Negro Leagues*. New York: Atheneum, 1965.

Rubin, Bob. *Satchel Paige: All-time Baseball Great*. New York: Putnam, 1974.

Ruck, Rob. *Sandlot Seasons: Sports in Black Pittsburgh*. Urbana: University of Illinois Press, 1987.

Rust, Art, Jr. *Get That Nigger Off the Field*. Los Angeles: Shadow Lawn Press, 1992.

Scott, Richard. *Jackie Robinson*. New York: Chelsea House, 1987.

Tygiel, Jules. *Baseball's Great Experiment: Jackie Robinson and His Legacy*. New York: Oxford University Press, 1983.

Veeck, Bill with Ed Linn. *Veeck as in Wreck*. New York: Putnam, 1972.

INDEX

Aaron, Henry, 85
Águilas club, 54
American Association, 90
American League, 15, 22, 65, 73, 81
Appling, Luke, 20, 22
Armstrong, Louis, 27
Atlanta Braves, 85
Atlanta Crackers, 42

Baird, Tom, 59, 62, 69
Baltimore Orioles, 75
Bankhead, Sam, 54
Barnstorming, 18, 26, 50, 83, 92
Baseball Hall of Fame, 20, 23, 48, 87–89
Bee Ball, 19, 37, 40
Bell, James ("Cool Papa"), 17, 39, 46, 52, 53, 59, 65, 82, 88
Benjamin, Jerry, 63
Berra, Yogi, 88
Birmingham, Alabama, 42, 43, 52
Birmingham Black Barons, 42
Bismarck, North Dakota, 49, 52
Boston Braves, 23, 71
Boston Red Sox, 23, 65, 71, 82, 83
Boudreau, Lou, 12, 22, 68, 69, 70, 71
Breslin, Jimmy, 83
Brooklyn Dodgers, 17, 18, 65, 75
Broun, Heywood, 62
Buffalo Bisons, 80

Calloway, Cab, 78
Campanella, Roy, 18, 75, 88
Campaneris, Bert ("Campy"), 82
Charleston, Oscar, 17, 46
Chattanooga Black Lookouts, 40, 41, 42

Chicago White Sox, 12, 16, 20, 22, 70
Cleveland Indians, 11, 12, 13, 15, 16, 18, 19, 20, 22, 23, 28, 65, 67, 68, 71, 72
Cleveland News, 69
Columbus Clippers, 78, 79
Comiskey Park, 70
Cooperstown, New York, 87, 88, 90
Crutchfield, Jimmie, 43
Cuba, 52
Cuban League, 16

Dandridge, Ray, 88
Dean, Dizzy, 16, 26, 51, 65, 73, 87, 93
Detroit Tigers, 74
Dihigo, Martin, 17, 88
DiMaggio, Joe, 51
Doby, Larry, 18, 20, 22, 67
Dominican League, 16
Dominican Republic, 53, 54
Don't Look Back: The Satchel Paige Story, 90
Dragones. See Trujillo Dragones
Durango, Mexico, 81

Easterling, Howard, 63
East-West All-Star Game, 48
Eureka Gardens, 29, 35

Feller, Bob, 16, 67, 70, 87
Finley, Charles O., 81, 82, 83
Forbes Field, 63
Foster, Rube, 88

Gardner, Floyd ("Jelly"), 39
Garver, Ned, 72
Gatewood, Bill, 42
Gehringer, Charlie, 51

Gibson, Josh, 17, 46, 47, 50, 52, 54, 60, 61, 62, 63, 64, 65, 87, 88
Gosset, Louis, Jr., 90
Greenlee, Gus, 45, 48, 54, 55
Guayama, Puerto Rico, 60, 61

Harlem Globetrotters, 77, 81
Herman, Alex, 40, 42
Hines, Wilbur, 30
Hodges, Gil, 75
Homestead Grays, 45, 46, 47, 62, 63, 74, 92
Hornsby, Rogers, 73, 74

Indianapolis Clowns, 81
Industrial School for Negro Children, 32, 36
International League, 77, 79
Irvin, Monte, 88, 92

Jim Crow laws, 20
Johnson, Judy, 46, 88
Jones, Slim, 48

Kansas City, Missouri, 90, 92
Kansas City Athletics, 77, 81, 83
Kansas City Monarchs, 17, 59, 60, 62, 65, 69, 72, 77, 90
Keltner, Ken, 22
Koufax, Sandy, 88

Latin America, 52
Latin leagues, 47, 50, 62
Lemon, Bob, 22, 69, 70
Leonard, Buck, 17, 63, 64, 88, 92
Lewis, John Henry, 46
Life, 61
Little League, 92

London, Julie, 81

Mathews, Eddie, 75
Maybe I'll Pitch Forever, 12, 90
Mays, Willie, 42
Mexican League, 16, 57
Mexico, 55, 57, 58
Miami Marlins, 77–81
Milwaukee Braves, 75
Minot Mallards, 77
Mitchum, Robert, 81
Mobile, Alabama, 25, 26, 28, 29, 31, 32, 33, 35, 59, 85, 90
Mobile Bears, 36, 37
Mobile's Down the Bay Boys, 39
Mobile Tigers, 29, 35, 36, 37, 39
Montreal Royals, 18, 78, 80
Mount Meigs, Alabama, 32, 33, 36
Municipal Stadium, 12, 14, 15
Musial, Stan, 48

National League, 18, 71, 73, 74
Negro American League, 42
Negro leagues, 13, 15, 16, 17, 18, 20, 26, 41, 45, 47, 48, 50, 51, 52, 53, 58, 61, 62, 67, 72, 75, 81, 82, 87, 88, 90, 92
Negro National League, 48, 52, 59, 63
Negro Southern League, 40
Newark Eagles, 55, 62, 67
New Orleans, Louisiana, 54
New Orleans Black Pelicans, 41
New Orleans Pelicans, 90
New York Cubans, 52
New York Yankees, 68, 71, 73

Old Timers' Club, 88–90

Pacific Coast League, 81
Paige, Carolyn Lahoma (daughter), 68
Paige, Janet Howard (first wife), 48, 58
Paige, John (father), 28
Paige, Lahoma Brown (second wife), 68, 81, 92
Paige, LeRoy ("Satchel")
    as an American League all-star, 74–75
    birth, 28
    childhood, 25–33
    death, 92
    early career, 35–39
    and the Hall of Fame, 20, 23, 48, 87–89
    and the major leagues, 11–23, 68–75, 81–85
    marriages, 48, 68
    and the minor leagues, 77–81
    and the Negro leagues, 35–55, 59–65
    receives nickname, 25–27
    in reform school, 31–33
    salaries, 36, 40, 41, 42, 48, 49, 50, 54–55, 65, 69, 83
    in the World Series, 23, 71
Paige, Linda Sue (daughter), 68
Paige, Lula Ouida (daughter), 68
Paige, Lulu (mother), 28, 32, 35
Paige, Pamela Jean (daughter), 68
Paige, Rita Jean (daughter), 68
Paige, Robert LeRoy (son), 68
Paige, Wilson (brother), 35, 36
Pegler, Westbrook, 62
Pittsburgh, Pennsylvania, 45, 48, 54
Pittsburgh Courier, 45, 46

Pittsburgh Crawfords, 45, 48, 49, 52
Pittsburgh Pirates, 75
Philadelphia Phillies, 65, 68
Portland Beavers, 81
Puerto Rican League, 61

Radcliffe, Ted ("Double Duty"), 49
Rickey, Branch, 18, 65
Robinson, Jackie, 17, 18, 65
Rochester Red Wings, 78, 80
Running Deer, Dorothy, 57
Ruth, Babe, 47, 50

St. Louis Browns, 28, 69, 72, 73, 74, 75
St. Louis Cardinals, 51, 75
St. Louis Stars, 39, 48
Satchel Paige's All-Stars, 59, 60
Saturday Evening Post, 61, 62
Slaughter, Enos, 75
Snider, Duke, 75
Sporting News, 28, 71

Time, 61
Trujillo Dragones, 53, 54
Trujillo Molina, Rafael, 53, 54

Veeck, Bill, 15, 19, 65, 67, 68, 71, 72, 75–79, 81, 83, 87

Washington Senators, 16, 69
W. H. Council School, 30–31
Whiting, Margaret, 78
Wilkinson, J. L., 59, 62
Williams, Ted, 23, 48, 71, 87
Wonderful Country, The, 81
Wynn, Early, 88

Yankee Stadium, 47, 48
Yastrzemski, Carl, 83

PICTURE CREDITS

————— ❦ —————

DAVID SHIRLEY is a freelance writer living in New York City. He is the author of *A Good Death* and is a frequent contributor to *Option Magazine*.

NATHAN IRVIN HUGGINS, one of America's leading scholars in the field of black studies, helped select the titles for the BLACK AMERICANS OF ACHIEVEMENT series, for which he also served as senior consulting editor. He was the W.E.B. Du Bois Professor of History and of Afro-American Studies at Harvard University and the director of the W.E.B. Du Bois Institute for Afro-American Research at Harvard. He received his doctorate from Harvard in 1962 and returned there as a professor in 1980 after teaching at Columbia University, the University of Massachusetts, Lake Forest College, and the California State University, Long Beach. He was the author of four books and dozens of articles, including *Black Odyssey: The Afro-American Ordeal in Slavery*, *The Harlem Renaissance*, and *Slave and Citizen: The Life of Frederick Douglass*, and was associated with the Children's Television Workshop, National Public Radio, the Boston Athenaeum, the Museum of Afro-American History, the Howard Thurman Educational Trust, and Upward Bound. Professor Huggins died in 1989, at the age of 62, in Cambridge, Massachusetts.